PRAISE FOR
HOLY GRAIL OF MARKETING

"Licciardi's book is a GPS for navigating the modern marketing world and arriving at higher ROIs faster."

—GLENN ROGINSKI, DIRECTOR,
INTEGRATED MEDIA STRATEGY AT PFIZER

"The code is cracked! *Holy Grail of Marketing* delivers a powerful framework that instantly uplevels any marketer's game. A big congrats to Greg Licciardi on writing a must-read for anyone ready to amplify their exposure."

—MIKE MICHALOWICZ, AUTHOR OF
PROFIT FIRST AND *GET DIFFERENT:
MARKETING THAT CAN'T BE IGNORED!*

"To succeed in today's markets, the product needs to be good but the message needs to be great. Knowing who you are talking to and what you are trying to say is the difference between success and failure. *Holy Grail of Marketing* lays this out in clear steps."

—TOM GILLIS, SENIOR VICE PRESIDENT/
GENERAL MANAGER INTERNET AND CLOUD
INFRASTRUCTURE AT CISCO SYSTEMS, INC.

"A slam dunk for anyone looking to turn marketing theory into real-world wins. As an associate professor of marketing at Seton Hall, where we prioritize practical education, I see this book as a gold mine for students and pros alike. It is packed with case studies and a logical framework that cuts through the clutter. I think of it as the playbook marketers need to score big in today's chaotic game."

—STEVE PIROG, ASSOCIATE PROFESSOR
AND FORMER MARKETING CHAIR, STILLMAN
SCHOOL OF BUSINESS, SETON HALL UNIVERSITY

"*Holy Grail of Marketing* is a one-of-a-kind treasure that redefines the landscape of modern marketing with its in-depth case studies, innovative strategies, and insightful analysis, leaving all pretenders in its wake. Any one claiming that they've 'already got one,' like the French guards in *Monty Python and The Holy Grail*, will be missing out. Dive into this groundbreaking book and discover why it's the only true Holy Grail of Marketing."

—JOE GAWRONSKI, CEO,
ROSENBLATT SECURITIES

"You can no longer invoke the old cliché 'Half of my advertising doesn't work, but I don't know which half.' In today's performance-based world, you have to know. Licciardi's *Holy Grail of Marketing* will show you how."

—BILL BRAZELL, PARTNER,
WIT STRATEGY

"This is an essential book for today's marketers, not only for its wisdom but how to put it into practice. Greg puts a spotlight on key elements of successful marketing that are often overlooked: targeting the right people based on demographic distinctions AND, most importantly, on attitudinal motivations; and creating the right emotionally motivating content unique to each platform."

—BRENT MAGID, PRESIDENT AND CEO, MAGID

"A masterpiece of marketing best practice!"

—MICKEY ALAM KHAN, CEO,
LUXURY ROUNDTABLE

"*Holy Grail of Marketing* is the perfect combination of an academic and theoretical perspective with a real-life application. The book is full of essential insights. It delivers a holistic approach that is applicable worldwide!"

—LUCA BIANCO, PRIVATE EQUITY
ANALYST, MCKINSEY & COMPANY
AND FORMER FORDHAM STUDENT

"The difference between good and great is not necessarily just skill, it's will. The passion to want to be great. This is a great read for anyone looking to unlock the marketing superhero they have inside their own self."

—DOUG ZARKIN, RETAIL AND BRAND MARKETING
EXPERT AND AUTHOR OF *MOVING YOUR
BRAND OUT OF THE FRIEND ZONE*

"Game-changer for modern marketers! *Holy Grail of Marketing* demystifies how to align data, AI, and strategy to drive real results. A sharp and highly practical read for anyone looking to optimize their marketing investments and outpace the competition."

—RICH SPIES, DIVERSIFIED
COMMUNICATIONS

"Greg Licciardi's *Holy Grail of Marketing* is essential reading in today's complex and rapidly evolving world of AI. His work provides a clear road map for marketers and business executives seeking a step-by-step approach to effectively target their customers. It's an easy yet comprehensive read, filled with detailed case studies that offer readers a master class in marketing."

—RICHARD SHAPIRO, FOUNDER
AND PRESIDENT, THE CENTER
FOR CLIENT RETENTION

"A simplified approach to the world of modern marketing. Success in today's rapidly evolving landscape requires blending data-driven insights with emotional brand connections to achieve lasting impact. This book presents a practical framework, supported by real-life case studies, to help navigate current challenges and unlock brand growth with actionable strategies, relevant tools, and effective measurement."

—JENNIFER PISCIOTTA, GLOBAL
VP MARKETING, D'USSE

"Understanding how your audience consumes media is more important than ever. This requires a structured approach with an understanding of the new media landscape. *Holy Grail of Marketing* breaks it all down in a simple way, so readers can easily navigate the complexities and take action with confidence."

—DAN DONNELLY, HEAD OF SPORTS
STRATEGY AT VIDEOAMP

"Today's marketing landscape is all about how to use new technologies effectively to connect with consumers and communicate the message. Greg digs deep into the art of so-called 'adtech' with case studies from leading brands Apple and LVMH."

—REBECCA FANNIN, FOUR-TIME AUTHOR
AND FOUNDER, SILICON DRAGON VENTURES

"Greg Licciardi masterfully marries high-tech with high-touch, reminding us that even in the age of AI-driven digital marketing, emotional connection remains paramount. With a perfect blend of art and science, he demystifies the *Holy Grail of Marketing*, offering a blueprint for success for our next generation of marketers."

—CHRIS J. BATTAGLIA, FOUNDER &
CEO, PARETO PARTNERS LLC

"The great brands don't just sell—they connect. *Holy Grail of Marketing* unpacks the art and science of reaching the right people with the right message at the right time. A must-read for anyone looking to build marketing that truly moves people."

"Holy Grail of Marketing is a must-read for marketers navigating today's fast-changing landscape. With real-world case studies, it highlights the power of AI, data, and emotional connection in driving brand success. This book is an invaluable guide to maximizing marketing impact and ROI. Highly recommended!"

"Optimizing every single dollar toward consumers with huge lifetime value is essential. In this enlightening book, Greg shows the way."

"As AI disrupts the way consumers operate, trusted brands can capture more value. Learn how the best modern marketers build brands and deliver winning results."

"A refreshing take on marketing, relatable at any level—a timely primer for the new AI era."

"The *Holy Grail of Marketing* is a must-read for every business person. The book presents a simplified approach to data-driven marketing strategies that are not only effective, but easy to comprehend in the fast-moving marketing field that has become more complicated with the increase of communication channels to reach the target consumer."

—JASON BERGMAN, CEO AT
AXIS GLOBAL LOGISTICS

HOLY GRAIL

of

MARKETING

HOLY GRAIL

of

MARKETING

How to Achieve Optimal
Marketing Using AI & Beyond

GREG P. LICCIARDI

www.holygrailofmarketing.com

IngramSpark

Interior design by THE COSMIC LION
Cover design by Adam Bohannon

Book title, *Holy Grail of Marketing*

First edition 2025

www.holygrailofmarketing.com

ISBN 979-8-9924930-0-9
ISBN 979-8-9924930-1-6 (ebook)

Contents

CONTENTS

Acknowledgments

This book would not have been possible without my soul mate and wife, Kristen, along with my amazing three boys, Gregory, Leo, and Daniel. Thank you for allowing me to follow my passion for teaching marketing with many late nights in the classroom and grading papers over the past ten years. You have also played a big part in sharing feedback and supporting me with publishing my book. This would not be possible without your amazing support and love.

A big thank you to my parents, Thomas and Paula Licciardi, who have always provided me with unwavering support to go beyond the normal and to follow my passions and dreams. I also want to recognize my six siblings—Fred, Tom, Pia, Chris, Marc, and Kevin—for supporting me, especially through life's not-always-easy times. My parents were big supporters of getting a good education with all seven kids graduating from Rutgers University.

ACKNOWLEDGMENTS

My father-in-law, Francis Kelly, is also an author and a child psychologist who was an inspiration to me in writing my book. My late mother-in-law, Susan Kelly Lions, also guided me in spirit.

Special thanks to Jill Davison, who helped launch my book by editing some of its early chapters. Jill is a marketing genius and a good friend who worked with me at American Express and went on to achieve greatness at other brands, including Mastercard. When I told Jill about my book concept more than a year and a half ago, she said, "Let's go! I would love to help make this the must-read modern-day marketing book you envision it to be." Thank you so much, Jill!

Fredric Nachbaur from Fordham Press, an extraordinary book publishing executive, provided invaluable advice and connected me with my final book editor, interior designer, and cover designer.

This book was edited and designed by an all-star team! Thank you, Lis, Lewelin, and Adam, for your amazing work:

- Lis Pearson, Book Editor
- Lewelin Polanco, Interior Book Designer and Founder of THE COSMIC LION
- Adam Bohannon, Cover Designer

My cousin, Howard Belger, and his partner, Christina Gillis, were great supporters. From the very beginning, they made many introductions, including Christina's cousin, John Gillis, who became one of my book's contributors.

I must also thank my good friend, Nuno and Al Greco from Fordham, who provided invaluable insights on the book's topic and book publishing.

Finally, I want to recognize and thank my Integrated Marketing Communications Fordham Spring 2025 class. The students in this class were remarkable and the first to read content from *Holy Grail of Marketing*. Throughout the semester, I assigned completed chapters, and the students provided insightful feedback, which has contributed to the success of *Holy Grail of Marketing*.

Contributors

Thank you to my amazing contributors for your
expertise and enthusiasm for my book.

MATTEO ATTI, Global Chief Marketing Officer at Vista Global, VistaJet, and XO.

PAULINE BROWN, former North America CEO at LVMH. Currently the founder of strategic advisory and branding firm, Aesthetic Intelligence Labs and author of award-winning book, *Aesthetic Intelligence: How to Boost It and Use It in Business and Beyond.*

JILL DAVISON is an accomplished global communications and brand marketing executive known for shaping impactful narratives and strategies across media, payments, and luxury lifestyle sectors.

BILL DUGGAN, Group EVP at the ANA (Association of National Advertisers), www.ana.net.

DAVID DESOCIO, EVP, Ad Sales Marketing and Partnerships at A+E Global Media which is home to some of the most popular and culturally relevant brands in media, including A&E®, Lifetime®, The HISTORY Channel™, LMN®, FYI®, Home.Made.Nation,™ and VICE TV®.

JOHN GILLIS, former Director of digital products at Harry's Razors. Climate entrepreneur and investor.

JONAH GOODHART, Co-Founder and CEO of Mobian. Previously, Jonah was the Co-Founder and CEO of Moat (acquired by Oracle) and founding investor in Right Media (acquired by Yahoo). Jonah is also a partner in WGI Group, an investment group with over 100 investments in the technology space.

LORI HAMILTON, Founder and President of Prosperity Productions, Inc. Insights expert, professor, innovator, strategist, marketer, writer.

VERA HSU, Director, AI/Data Platform GTM at Microsoft.

SHELLY KOHAN, top 100 global retail influencer, professor, podcaster, retail pundit, and speaker.

SERTAN KABADAYI, Professor of marketing at Fordham Gabelli School of Business.

PHILLIP LOMAX, EVP, MediaScience where he leads strategic growth initiatives empowering brands and media companies with actionable insights grounded in cutting-edge consumer neuroscience.

JIM MCCANN, Founder and CEO of 1-800 Flowers and owner of Harry & David.

SARA MELEFSKY, Marketing Campaign Strategist at JR Automation.

ANASTASIA PARANICAS, Expert in consumer packaged goods (CPG) marketing, innovation, e-commerce, and start-ups with experience working for emerging and leading brands at Unilever, Post Foods, and Church & Dwight.

ADAM QUINN, SVP of Strategic Accounts at Simulmedia which harnesses the power of data and AI to deliver strategic TV audiences with precision targeting and high engagement.

RANDI STIPES, Chief Marketing Officer at The Weather Company which is a leading weather forecasting and information technology company that owns and operates weather.com and Weather Underground.

CAN USLAY, Professor of Marketing at Rutgers Business School.

JAMES WRIGHT, Executive Director at Interbrand which is a leading global brand consultancy involving strategy and design.

HOLY GRAIL

of

MARKETING

Introduction

Picture this. It's Wednesday, my work-from-home day, and I'm at my computer in my home office. It's nearly noon, and I feel hungry. I want a chicken sandwich from my favorite fast-food restaurant, Wendy's, so I quickly finish what I'm doing, grab my keys, and in no time I'm at the Wendy's kiosk ordering a chicken sandwich just as I like it—a classic chicken sandwich combo with pickles, lettuce, tomato, and mayo. I pick it up, pay at the register, head home, and enjoy my perfect meal.

A week later, I'm back working in my home office. It's mid-morning when I receive a message on my Facebook feed from, you guessed it, Wendy's. They're reaching out about that delicious chicken sandwich I had the week before as I take a quick break from my calls to check my social feed. The ad arrives before I've even contemplated today's lunch, with an offer that can't be beat. This time I order my sandwich before heading to Wendy's drive-through. I love the timely lunch reminder, and the savings, and I'm salivating for that chicken sandwich. I now get special offers from Wendy's every Wednesday morning, reminding me that my perfect meal is waiting for me.

Wendy's is reaching the right person, with the right message, in the right environment, at the right time, and the right outcome is achieved, $$$!

This is the power of achieving the Holy Grail of Marketing—this book's foundation.

Whether it's Wendy's or another brand marketing to me, achieving the Holy Grail of Marketing is the most effective approach for successfully capturing consumers' attention, trust, loyalty, and dollars.

Marketing is the "why" we emotionally connect with brands. Think about it: What brands and products are you buying and why? Did you buy a particular can of soup on your last trip to the grocery store? How about mustard, ketchup, or another condiment? What about the last time you purchased an automobile or booked a vacation? What destination, hotel, and airline did you choose? You chose that mustard brand or booked that hotel because of marketing.

Effective marketing makes a brand stand apart, stand tall, and be relevant. However, today's framework for effective marketing is becoming even more complex as the media landscape continues to fragment, with new and emerging technologies involving AI and digital applications increasing at a breakneck speed.

In our screen-obsessed world, the average American is exposed to 4,000–10,000 ads daily. Faced with constant messaging, people are easily annoyed, weary, and desensitized. They tune out, intentionally avoiding advertising.

For marketers, consumer ad fatigue translates into diminished engagement levels, lower click-through rates, and other indicators negatively impacting an ad campaign's overall performance. There's nothing worse for a brand than being ignored and considered irrelevant.

Marketers must create innovative, non-intrusive ways to build brand relevance and strengthen consumer engagement. That's why they must thoroughly understand sophisticated, data-driven techniques and tools to optimize resources, performance, and dollars.

As AI and other emerging new technologies disrupt marketing, brands must resist becoming commoditized by focusing on short-term optimized transactions. The more a brand emotionally connects with their desired audience, the more it succeeds. This will be covered in depth in Chapter 5 as I explore right outcomes with insights provided by one of my contributing editors, James Wright, from Interbrand a leading global brand consultancy.

I wrote *Holy Grail of Marketing* as a beacon for anyone launching a brand, big or small, and accountable for every marketing dollar they spend. My book is also designed for anyone passionate about succeeding in marketing, no matter the stage of their career.

I'll start by explaining the Holy Grail of Marketing and how this innovative framework can break down barriers to gain market share, whether you're building a start-up or are part of an established multibillion-dollar company.

I'll share each of the steps and explain how it is achieved by a brand's ability to:

Reach the Right Person
With the Right Message
In the Right Environment
At the Right Time
Delivering the Right Outcome

The Holy Grail of Marketing is optimized by data and AI. I'll demonstrate how data and insights can help you identify and understand your best existing and prospective customers. Utilizing the most sophisticated digital tools, such as AI, time-based data, near-field communication, social media, contextual targeting, and more, will be invaluable as you embark on creating and executing a successful marketing campaign.

For example, contextual messaging enables marketers to reach the right person at the right time with contextually relevant data designed to meet the individual's needs, desires, and interests at a specific time and delivered in the optimal environment. Optimization and personalization are critical.

I'll review the positive outcomes of this framework, so your brand appears in a safe environment and is not left behind. To help you avoid hazards, I'll also address when and how the Holy Grail of Marketing can backfire when the strategy isn't implemented effectively.

As AI and new marketing technologies accelerate the speed of change and complexity of the marketing landscape, the Holy Grail of Marketing provides a guiding framework to help marketers succeed.

With the rapid pace of change and marketers being increasingly dazzled by AI's automation, I'll emphasize how important it is for brands to maintain and grow the emotional connection they have with their consumers. Brand purpose will increasingly be important to maintaining a brand's lifetime value.

Finally, I'll share some powerful case studies illustrating when and how the Holy Grail of Marketing can be optimally achieved, creating optimal value and success.

Opening Prospectus from the Association of National Advertisers (ANA)

"How do you build a brand?" That's such a simple question. But if you ask ten different Chief Marketing Officers (CMOs), you'll get ten different responses. It's a bit like asking an artist, "How do you paint a painting?"

Of course, you need a product or service. And that product or service needs to be conveniently available to the customer either in a physical location or via e-commerce—ideally both. And the pricing for that product or service needs to be appropriate. Then, there is the communication and there are many ways to develop communication to build a brand. This book provides the framework for doing just that.

In cinema, Indiana Jones famously searched for the Holy Grail—the cup that Jesus and his apostles drank from during the Last Supper. I'll provide you with a framework for achieving the Holy Grail of Marketing—*reaching the right person with the right message in the right environment at the right time and the right outcome is delivered.*

The beauty of the Holy Grail of Marketing is its simplicity, which provides structure and calm over the complicated and fragmented world of marketing. In today's environment, where marketing is harder than ever, the smartest marketers pay special attention to:

- **Reaching the Right Person:** This demands inclusive marketing. The United States is increasingly diverse and multiracial; the multicultural population was 42.2 percent in the 2020 census and is certainly more today (half the children born in America today are from a diverse background). Marketers need to recognize the power of inclusive marketing and that includes the LGBTQ+ community.

- **With the Right Message:** ANA research shows that "a tight brief with clearly defined objectives" is the number-one ranked enabler of great creative work by both marketers and agencies. Meanwhile, "poor creative briefs—lacking in focus and clarity" is a top roadblock to achieving creativity objectives, again per both marketers and agencies. Developing the right message begins with the creative brief.

- **In the Right Environment:** Today, most advertising dollars are spent on digital media and most digital is bought programmatically. And often, programmatic advertising appears on an insane number of websites. According to the ANA 2023 Programmatic Media Supply Chain Transparency report, the average advertiser in that study was on 44,000 websites. Yikes! Bad things can happen when ads run on the wrong sites—there could be brand safety issues, increased likelihood for ad fraud, and the possibility that the ad might not even be viewable. Context—i.e., the right environment—matters!

- **At the Right Time:** We live in an always-on marketing environment; think about the speed and influence of social media. Marketers must be prepared to communicate both proactively and in response to real-time issues. Increasingly, we are seeing companies take some agency services in-house, especially those dependent on quick turnaround time—like social media specifically.

- **The Right Outcome is Delivered:** There is a saying in marketing credited to educator and author Peter Drucker, "What gets measured gets managed and improved." Data can be a marketer's best friend. Measuring marketing performance, of course, leads to the evaluation, and often improvement, of the marketing which then leads to better outcomes.

So, how do you build a brand? While ten different CMOs will provide ten different responses, the framework for achieving the Holy Grail of Marketing would most likely be a common denominator among those responses—*reaching the right person with the right message in the right environment at the right time and the right outcome is delivered.*

Bill Duggan

Group EVP
ANA (Association of National Advertisers) – www.ana.net

The Holy Grail of Marketing

*How Brands are Using It to Break Down Barriers and
Market Share from Multibillion-Dollar Companies*

I often include improv exercises in my classes because they are the most effective way to teach and learn. So, let's kick this book off with one. Imagine you were just given a marketing budget. This budget could have come from your boss, a private equity firm, or perhaps from your own savings. The budget size and where it comes from don't

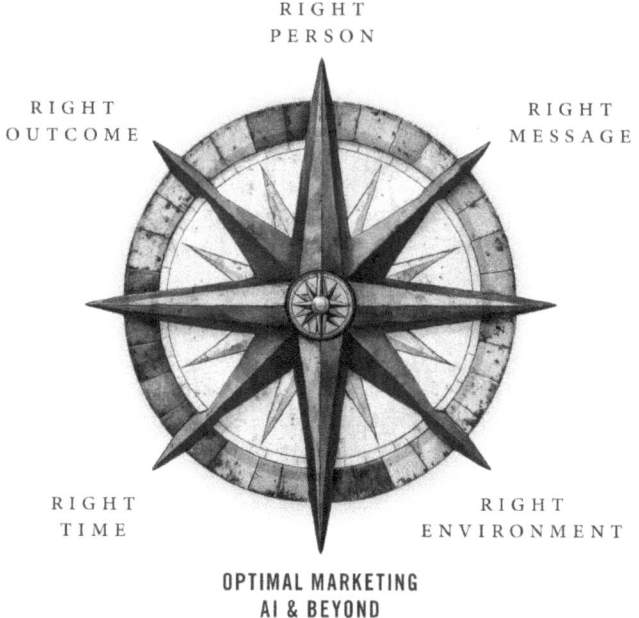

RIGHT
PERSON

RIGHT
OUTCOME

RIGHT
MESSAGE

RIGHT
TIME

RIGHT
ENVIRONMENT

OPTIMAL MARKETING
AI & BEYOND

matter. Over the following two hundred pages of this book you'll see that what matters most is that no matter where your funds come from, you're accountable for every dollar you spend. Let's take it a step further: for every dollar you invest in marketing that's not going toward the growth of your brand, business, or service, you'll miss out on an opportunity to gain increased sales and market share. You might also risk losing your job or the dream business you launched.

Now that we have set the playing field, let's have some fun and dive in! To plan a successful marketing campaign that delivers a positive return on investment (ROI), what are some of the most important elements you'll need to focus on to succeed? Pause and take some time to think about this.

I recommend closing this book and closing your eyes to reflect on this. Think about a campaign you've been impressed by—what made it work so well? See you back here in twenty minutes.

WHAT IS THE WHITE SPACE
YOU ARE CAPTURING?

Welcome back. Allow me to help share some thought-starters. What's the white space in the marketplace where there is an unfulfilled consumer need not being met? Whose attention are you trying to capture? What need are you trying to fulfill? Next, think about the consumer or business that's most in need of your product or service. Everything in your marketing campaign will stem from this. So, before we leave the gate and start developing ads and spending media dollars, make sure you're clear on who the right person is to whom you will direct a large majority of your marketing funds.

You need to know intimately who your core customer is to achieve the ROI you set out to accomplish with every dollar you invest in marketing. I'll help you explore this further through other exercises and analyses later in this book.

Let's keep going. What else is essential once you fully understand who your most important customer is? What's your unique selling proposition (USP)? What's your brand's purpose? What's your brand's core DNA and how will it enhance a person's life? How is your product or service unique in fulfilling your target audience's unmet need? The right message can't be achieved without understanding what makes a consumer interested, attentive, and willing to click through. Knowing what motivates this person is essential. Your message should embody and take advantage of this knowledge.

Let's keep going! Now that you have the right person and message, what else is necessary to make your campaign excel? Feel free to take another break—go for a walk or get a bowl of your favorite ice cream—whatever helps get your creative juices flowing.

Ok, I hope you've come back to a place where you are not distracted and are able to focus.

Once you have crystalized your message, you'll want it to appear in a high-engagement environment that supports and enhances your marketing message. The most effective environment is one that is contextually relevant to both your message and the person receiving it.

For example, a new dog owner might be interested in a list of Fourth of July dog safety tips. That list could be brought to you by Purina and featured in the *Puppy Times* newsletter—sent to people who have purchased a dog within the past six months.

Ok, take another break. Maybe take your dog—or yourself—for a quick walk.

Welcome back. I hope this is a good time and I have your full attention. Did I say time? Yes, the timing of your message is paramount! The right time is when the person you are sending your message to is captivated, undistracted, and as close as possible to the time they need and desire to purchase what you are selling to them. We don't want to sell wedding rings to already married couples. We don't want to sell ski products in July. What if we were launching website for dog products? We would only want to target dog owners. However, a new survey states that most dog product purchases happen within the first six months of ownership. This added insight enables us to focus on *new* dog owners when the timing is optimal for them to purchase our products.

TIMING YOUR MESSAGE MATTERS

As I shared in my introduction, timing matters, as seen from my Wendy's example. Up to this point, we have identified that reaching the right person with the right message at the right time will optimize the effectiveness and ROI of our marketing investment. However, another critical aspect to a successful marketing campaign is often overlooked. Think about where your message is delivered. It might have great timing, but what if it ends up being shown on a fraudulent website or a streaming program that does not reflect your brand's ethos and message? What if your ad appears on a site not culturally relevant to your target audience? What if you just produced a new video ad shown on X with very few views when it could have appeared on TikTok and Instagram with far greater engagement?

DELIVERING THE RIGHT OUTCOME

Ultimately, you want your campaign to deliver the right outcome that is measurable, profitable, and aligned with the outcome you are setting out to achieve. We will drill down on this in Chapter 10.

MARKETING EVOLUTION

My marketing experience began when I was fresh out of college selling *Yellow Pages* (printed phone book directory) ads. This provided me with a front-row seat to the power of advertising. I consulted with companies on expanding their storefront by adding listings under an associated heading (think Google ad words). For example, a glass repair shop could be listed under several headings, such as glass, glass repair, and home improvement. A business's regional footprint could instantly expand by adding an ad in a neighboring town's directory (think of geo-segmentation or geo-targeting used today for digital advertising placements).

The *Yellow Pages* taught me everything I needed to know about marketing at the time. Little did I know that it would prepare me for a massively changing world. With today's vast ecosystem of new and emerging data-driven technologies, businesses have infinite choices when it comes to marketing. While you could say the changes have been evolutionary, you'd also be correct if you described the transformation as revolutionary. Let's examine how the marketing function got to where it is today.

Marketing messages have been around since the beginning of time. Remember the hieroglyphics and cave drawings we learned about in grade school? People were exposed to these communication symbols in ancient civilizations. Fast forward to the nineteenth and twentieth centuries, when mass media, including newspapers, magazines, broadcast television, and radio, led the way for brand awareness.

One such campaign epitomizing advertising in the age of mass media was the iconic 1950s Volkswagen Beetle ad by Doyle Dane Bernbach (DDB) that featured the new automobile from Volkswagen with a photograph of the car, and clever, humorous, long-form copy under the heading, "Think Small." The only measured sentiment was how cool and creative the advertisement was. DDB was credited with the greatest ad of all time in 1959, as agencies were evaluated by the creative and likability of the ads, not by the business outcome.

Creating awareness is critical, but modern-day marketers need to demonstrate ROI. As John Wanamaker, considered one of the pioneers of modern marketing, famously said, "Half the money I spend on advertising is wasted; the trouble is I don't know which half?" The question wouldn't be answered until the early 2000s when the digital age loomed and began delivering precise, measurable, data and science.

ACCOUNTABILITY LEADS THE WAY

With the help of cutting-edge technology, gone were the days of placing an ad and hoping to sell something to someone. Today's marketers are responsible for reaching the right audience, converting them into leads, and, ultimately, sales. What's more, these are cost-effective techniques in a modern marketer's toolbox. Nearly every tactic, from advertising performance to social media campaigns, is proven through advanced measurement tools. Marketers use all these tech-driven—quantitative and qualitative—capabilities to help identify and build customer relationships and drive sales, revenue, and profitability. Now more than ever, chief marketing officers (CMOs) and their teams are held accountable for demonstrating tangible business results and ROI.

The average tenure for a CMO today is just 3.5 years. Why is this? Because today they're accountable for every marketing dollar invested and responsible for their company making their quarterly revenue forecasts. Four missed quarters can result in termination. CMOs must also keep up with the latest trends and technologies, or they will fall behind and be replaced by marketing professionals who are better educated and equipped with the experience and skills needed.

MODERN-DAY MARKETING IS INTERDISCIPLINARY

The marketing classes I teach often involve marketing, technology, finance, and analytics students. Marketing today is multifaceted. Many CMOs today have a technology background, which helps them select the most effective marketing technologies to automate and optimize their campaigns. Universities have adjusted their curriculums to include classes, majors, and master's degrees focused on marketing intelligence and analytics. MBA degrees are more valuable than ever as they contain a multifaceted curriculum. A successful marketing professional today needs to be able to work across several departments in addition to marketing, including research, consumer insights, technology, finance, and ad creative development. MBA curriculums also include classes on influencer marketing and social media. However, a student who wants to enhance their viability to enter a marketing career also has an option to get a master's degree in Marketing Intelligence, which is usually half the credits needed to earn an MBA.

With executives questioning the impact of marketing, it's critical for practitioners to keep pace and understand the new technologies which enable them to collect, analyze, and interpret vast amounts of data in real time. This information provides insights into customer behavior, preferences, and trends, allowing businesses to make informed decisions. From this enormous data collection and analysis, marketers can glean insights into an endless treasure trove of consumer mindsets, behaviors, preferences, trends, and more.

GARBAGE IN, GARBAGE OUT

Although these insights help power efficient and consistent campaigns, human marketing practitioners are in the driver's seat when analyzing the data, identifying and interpreting the insights, and creating strategic direction and action. Data is only as good as the marketing talent who keenly understands it and can put it into play effectively. This can't be understated. AI is making it easier to get more timely data. However, as the saying goes—"garbage in, garbage out." Marketing professionals need to be skilled at producing input queries that align with the sought-after output. Marketers also need to be able to interpret data and create insights in a storytelling format that their internal teams and outside partners will clearly understand.

The internet would change media and advertising to an "always on," data-driven, omnichannel paradigm, which AI is increasingly optimizing. Think mobile, social, real-time location tech, contextual advertising, and more.

THE CONSUMER IS KING

Today, people are bombarded with messaging 24/7 on every channel and all their devices—whenever and wherever they are. Data-driven tech—AI, IoT, wearables, 5G, AR, VR—will continue to advance. So, too, will the marketing function experience historic growth and transformation at an unmatched, accelerated pace.

The consumer today is king—they hold all the cards. They're in charge and in control. Watching media on their mobile devices all the time. Wherever/whenever. Their entertainment system goes with them everywhere. They scroll their feeds in TikTok, sports score, and IG in a matter

of seconds. Marketers need to find these customers where they are consuming media. This practice harnesses data, AI, and other advanced technologies to determine consumers' needs and desires. It's about reaching the *right person* with the *right message* in the *right environment* at the *right time* with the *right outcome*. To optimize and achieve the Holy Grail of Marketing it's important to know where your targeted consumer is within their consumer journey.

CALIBRATE YOUR MARKETING TO WHERE YOUR CONSUMER IS IN THEIR JOURNEY

If you are marketing a new product with mass appeal and your main goal is to raise awareness of your brand, you will want to activate the top of the consumer journey/marketing funnel (see figure below) that delivers the broadest reach. Think Super Bowl ads on network TV. If you want to move your consumer from consideration to preference, you will need to develop messaging that educates the consumer on why your brand is key to delivering on their needs and desires.

If you are looking at your next quarter's numbers and you see that sales are slipping, you'll likely have to shift marketing dollars toward the bottom of the funnel with activities to increase conversions/sales. Some of these efforts

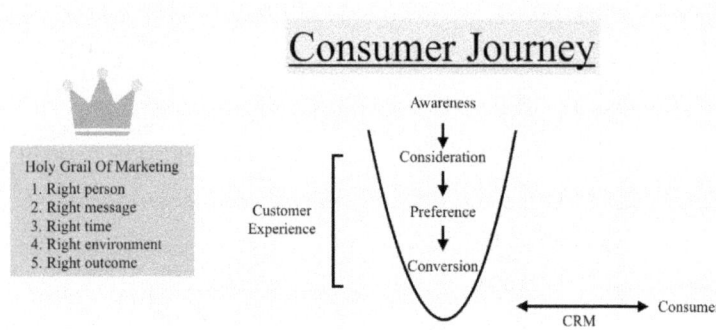

could include promotions with coupons through newsletters, direct mail, or point of sale (POS) in retail locations. You might also want to look at how to increase sales from current customers who have purchased from you in the past. This is where you will activate your customer relationship marketing (CRM) efforts to embrace your most loyal customers. This is where brands should focus on the 80/20 rule: 20 percent of your customers deliver 80 percent of your sales. So, if you're selling diapers you will want to send special coupons to your bulk-purchasing consumers to incentivize them to buy more, now.

After determining the right person, the contextually relevant message is as imperative as the environment. This is what makes or breaks the customer experience, resulting in a positive or negative impression of your brand.

HOW A START-UP USED DATA-DRIVEN INSIGHTS TO ACHIEVE THE HOLY GRAIL OF MARKETING

How can a start-up break into an established category, rapidly removing barriers, alleviating consumer pain points, and successfully disrupting a multibillion-dollar sector? The odds seem impossible.

Unless you're Harry's—the trendy, direct-to-consumer shaving company founded by Jeffrey Raider, a cofounder of Warby Parker, and Andy Katz-Mayfield in 2013. The two entrepreneurs took on the P&G-owned giant Gillette, which at the time commanded more than 65 percent of the market share.

Harry's cracked the market with a subscription business boasting affordable, high-quality shaving solutions. In a matter of months, the company gained significant market share, becoming a competitive threat in the razor sector. Harry's would become a global powerhouse within five years with a whopping $1.7 billion valuation. Today, Harry's is a $400 million+ brand.

The company originated after Katz-Mayfield went shopping for a razor at his local pharmacy, leaving him uninspired by what he considered a dull product at an unreasonable price. After identifying this white space in the market, he and

Raider reimagined a high-quality shaving experience sold directly to consumers through convenient, affordable subscriptions.

Let's take a look at how Harry's came out of nowhere, with game-changing speed and success, utilizing the Holy Grail of Marketing:

Right Person

Harry's target audience was the urban millennial male in his 20s and 30s, interested in feeling and looking their best.

With a team of twelve employees, Harry's developed a savvy word-of-mouth referral engine. Each person contacted their respective network of friends and family, inviting them to Harry's landing page, where they opted in.

At the same time, Harry's created a simple game of prizes, building engagement and transforming their nucleus of early customers into a more extensive network. The more people they'd refer the more free prizes (swag!) they could win. For five referrals, they won free shaving cream; for twenty-five, a free shaving set; and for fifty, a grand prize of a one-year supply of razor blades. These incentives resulted in the network's growth to an incredible 100,000 email addresses of prequalified fans—before launch!

Harry's essentially led a grassroots campaign via gamification to build a referral engine. The audience, in turn, raised Harry's visibility and increased its brand awareness by leveraging word-of-mouth marketing.

Seventy-seven percent of the emails came from referrals, meaning approximately 20,000 people referred about 65,000 friends. This is referral marketing at its best, leveraging customers' satisfaction with products and services.

It's important to note that Harry's also generated backlinks through this network. The more backlinks were posted about Harry's, the more Harry's name and messaging around its products and experience were prioritized in SEO queries.

"In a virtuous circle, Harry's marketing strategy is defined by its customers, both the consumers and producers of their content. It may sound radical, but every team at Harry's is directly involved in speaking to our customers and finding out what makes them tick," explained Jenni Lee, former head of brand and marketing at Harry's (quote from Canva.com/learn), when describing the company's core audience.

Harry's succeeded at identifying and building strong connections with a loyal audience before launching its subscription service.

Right Message

Harry's had a story to tell. Their narrative—the right message—was core to their strategy from the get-go and fundamental to their success. Harry's focused on their core brand purpose to deliver an affordable, stylish razor to a young customer's home.

First, very few companies acknowledge that razors are expensive, but Harry's explicitly referenced the high cost of shaving in their marketing on their "About page." This recognition of price profoundly resonated with people because they agreed. Harry's reinforced the buyer persona's pain (expensive razor blades) and positioned itself as the innovative, stylish solution (custom-made razor blades at affordable prices).

Second, people love rooting for the underdog, and with a daunting uphill battle at launch, Harry's went head-to-head unapologetically with the category leader, Gillette. They positioned themselves as the new kid on the block, embracing their role as David to Gillette's Goliath.

Harry's articulated its underdog image consistently throughout its compelling advertising campaigns and earned media coverage. The positioning was also reinforced by customers' comments on both their own social channels and Harry's.

Harry's was selling an experience that combined shaving with style and affordability with story archetypes that resonated with people. Their narrative connected with consumers emotionally, giving them the information they needed to embrace Harry's.

"We remind ourselves to treat customers like our peers and speak to them like humans. Avoid treating people like a statistic or data point, as people want to be spoken to like another human or friend," explained Lee. "Our consumers are our biggest influence. We're constantly speaking to them to find out what they want if they have a problem to be solved or how they want to be communicated with."

Harry's succeeded in creating relatable, compelling storytelling that inspired and empowered people to become customer brand advocates.

Harry's marketing team created numerous photos, quick videos for social sharing, and language to tie it all together. A great example is the #ownyourAM hashtag on both Twitter and Facebook. This hit home the image of the peaceful, paradisiacal morning which resonated with Harry's customers!

Right Environment

Harry's strategically meets its target audience of young millennial men online—where they consume media. The company first reached this group primarily through the word-of-mouth referral network they built on social media platforms such as YouTube and Facebook.

Leveraging gamification tactics, Harry's drove consumer engagement with product giveaways. Harry's tapped into the power of its online network of loyal customers who evangelized the brand experience within its networks.

In addition to leveraging their brand ambassadors on social media, Harry's introduced a new product line exclusively at Target in 2016. It was no accident that they chose a mass-market retail distributor that shared a focus on reaching millennial, middle-class shoppers through the creation and curation of experiences.

Right Time

Reaching millennial men who care about value and price point was critical for Harry's but reaching them at the right time was equally important.

As discussed earlier in this chapter, people are bombarded with marketing messaging and ad clutter. Capturing consumer attention is challenging, so Harry's had to develop innovative, nonintrusive ways to connect with its target audience.

Creating content around significant, monumental cultural moments that reflected the brand's personality was how Harry's built and strengthened consumer engagement.

For example, Harry's launched National Shave Day on December 1, 2013, appealing to men who needed a good razor after not shaving during Movember. If you're unfamiliar with Movember, it's the annual event promoting the growth of mustaches during November to raise awareness of men's health issues.

Harry's rode the coattails of this cultural moment, and they created a message to appeal to their target audience in a timely, prescient, and actionable way. Men who didn't shave during Movember desperately needed a shave.

John Gillis who was the former director of digital products during Harry's early days shares, "It's interesting to think about 'excuses' to talk to people—everyone wants something to talk about. The more unique to your industry or brand something is, the more you can get away with turning a non-event into an event. For example, all Brands want to celebrate global impact events such as Pride or Valentine's Day but can you find a more authentic brand moment to start a conversation? E.g., Taco Tuesday. . . . The key to finding these appropriate moments always come from knowing your customer better and knowing what they care about."

Harry's story (right message) resonated with existing and prospective customers (right person)—but Harry's critical timing facilitated the demand for the product. As the saying goes, timing is everything. The company experienced a 360 percent increase in website traffic during this period.

Right Outcome

Harry's achieved the Holy Grail of Marketing, excelling at every step of the marketing process: a robust and authentic connection with the target audience (right person); compelling, emotional storytelling (right message); thoughtful and appropriate media (right environment); and a timely, even prescient moment that activates consumer behavior—think

bottom of the consumer journey/marketing funnel (right time). Together, the sum of these parts resulted in Harry's meeting and exceeding its revenue goals and catapulting the company into an industry giant and one of the most successful start-ups in history (right outcome).

Case Study: Cheat Sheet

Right Person. Harry's identified its target audience as millennial, price-conscious men who cared about feeling and looking good. To reach this group of individuals, the twelve-member launch team created a game for people to win prizes in order to build brand awareness and heighten consumer engagement. Their gamification tactics reflected referral marketing at its best, as Harry's built a referral network of 100,000 email sign-ups. Even before the product launch, Harry's identified a group of loyal brand ambassadors and evangelists. It reached the right person.

Right Message. After identifying white space in the shaving market, Raider and Katz-Mayfield developed an irreverent, anti-big razor narrative, breaking down significant barriers to entering an established category. The cofounders understood what people sought and wanted in the shaving

experience and assumed the underdog David to Gillette's Goliath. The emotional, relevant storytelling resonated with people. It was the right message.

Right Environment. To capture the attention of its buyers nonintrusively, Harry's meets its audience of young millennial men where they are—on their social media platforms. Since its introduction, Harry's has communicated to their target audience in a dialogue format. While the company created and distributed customized content for its consumers on its social feeds, Harry's also monitored their customers' feedback and brand sentiments, both the good and the bad. Harry's used social media to heighten brand awareness, strengthen engagement, and extend its loyal customer base. They found the right environment.

Right Time. After developing compelling storytelling and identifying the core consumer, Harry's sought the right moment to capture the audience's attention. With creativity and innovative thinking, the team created monumental moments pegged to pop culture, like the successfully executed National Shaving Day campaign, which increased significant traffic to its website, strengthening consumer engagement and sales.

Harry's also leveraged hyperpersonalization tactics by enhancing the shaving experience for a low price, honing the consumer journey. The company provided prospective buyers with various options when they wouldn't complete their online purchase, driving bottom-of-the-funnel marketing. Like the referral engine they built, Harry's offered incentives, such as a free product trial—they converted prospective customers into buyers at the right time.

Right Outcome. Harry's brilliantly achieved the Holy Grail of Marketing. Leveraging the right person with the right message in the right environment at the right time—they achieved the right outcome. The creation and implementation of these factors drove Harry's enormous, record-breaking success. Harry's strategic marketing activations and campaigns incorporated each of the steps above and together powered its unprecedented success. The Holy Grail of Marketing can only be achieved when all its parts are activated and optimized. Every step is necessary.

How AI and Data Optimize the Ability to Achieve the Holy Grail of Marketing

DATA AND TECHNOLOGY ARE EMPOWERING MARKETERS TO REACH THEIR CONSUMERS IN MORE MEANINGFUL WAYS

Marketers are increasingly being tapped to utilize and optimize the available tactics to drive a business's bottom line. While the 4Ps of the marketing mix—product, price, place, and promotion—continue to be utilized, technology and data have changed this strategic framework to be more consumer- and experience-centric. Understanding and using digital tools the right way is empowering advertisers to engage with existing and prospective customers in more meaningful, effective ways than they could have ever dreamed.

Combining the science and art of how we practice marketing today—reaching the *Right Person with the Right Message in the Right Environment at the Right Time with the Right Outcome*—is the North Star for delivering ROI.

A great deal is at stake for established brands and hungry start-ups. Data-driven tech enables new, start-up products and services to break through the clutter quickly, capturing significant sales and dollars in what were considered established markets, altering the landscape.

COMBINING SCIENCE AND ART
DELIVERS GAME-CHANGING RESULTS

Today's marketers have to integrate the left- and right-brained elements. As Philip Kotler, considered the father of modern marketing, explained, "marketing is the science and art of exploring, creating, and delivering value to satisfy the needs of a target market at a profit."

Let's look at a powerful example of how combining science and art can be put into action delivering game-changing results. What's one of the most powerful data triggers affecting consumer behavior? Have you checked the weather forecast lately? Half of Americans check the weather forecast daily according to a recent YouGov survey. Think about the last trip you took and how many packing and planning decisions were driven by the forecasted weather conditions. I recently had the pleasure of interviewing the CMO at The Weather Company who shared great insights on how they're helping marketers optimize their marketing campaigns through providing weather data and insights.

The Weather Company (formerly owned by IBM) is a global leader in weather data, forecasting, and insights. It's best known for its ownership of weather.com and The Weather Channel app and brand. What started as an idea in a basement studio has become one of the world's most trusted brands and the world's most accurate weather forecaster.

Since its inception nearly five decades ago, the company has combined human-meteorological expertise with innovative technology to drive progress. As the weather becomes more erratic, The Weather Company is helping businesses leverage weather data and insights to evolve and thrive as consumer behavior and expectations shift in a rapidly changing world.

WEATHER IS THE ORIGINAL INFLUENCER

"Weather is the original influencer—as great as Taylor Swift is these days, weather was there first," explains Randi Stipes, the company's CMO. "Think about your routine. Think about how much weather impacts your decisions, from the minute you wake up to the minute you go to bed: what to wear, what to eat, how you feel, what you plan, where you travel."

Stipes and her team utilize an agile, data-driven approach to drive business growth and deliver measurable results, tapping into the organization's massive historical, current, and forecasted weather datasets. This valuable trove of data and insights is crucial to The Weather Company's ability to help marketers make informed decisions about their campaigns. It delivers the right message to the right people at the right time through hyperlocal ads that encourage behavior based on the current weather's impact in that area.

Using weather data isn't just practical. It's privacy-safe and a critical consideration for marketers today as tracking cookies become deprecated and marketers are under scrutiny over their handling of sensitive PII data.

THE WEATHER COMPANY AND E.L.F. COSMETICS

e.l.f. Cosmetics turned to The Weather Company in 2022 for its highly effective, contextual targeting capabilities that would be the foundation for creating a viral, brand-building campaign centered around consumer behavior and emotions. The multibrand beauty company, with its range of vegan, cruelty-free beauty and personal care products, aimed to promote its brand's purpose of self-expression by creating a weather-driven strategy involving data-driven tech and innovative marketing tactics.

EIGHT IN TEN WOMEN WILL CHANGE THEIR BEAUTY ROUTINE BASED ON THE WEATHER

According to data uncovered by The Weather Company, eight in ten women say they change their beauty routines based on the weather. For e.l.f., this insight was game-changing and would become the foundation of their campaign, intended to reach young consumers.

"When you say an insight that 8 in 10 women will change their beauty routine because of the weather, how can you not lean in?" asked Vice President of Integrated Marketing Communications Patricia O'Keefe. "And lean in we did, with the e.l.f. Twist."

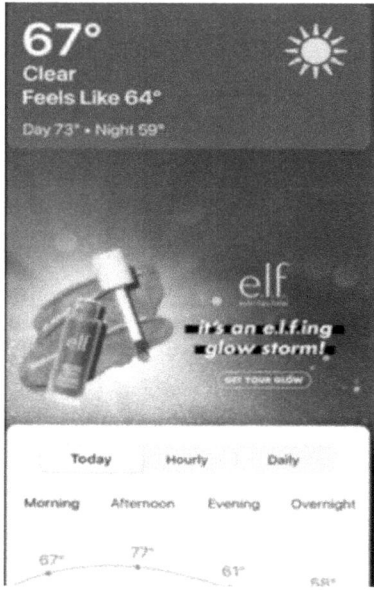

e.l.f. built a holiday-themed campaign around weather's relatability and relevance, promoting the restocking of its Halo Glow Primer product. The creative featured entertaining messages and animated images that promoted Halo Glow Primer, reflecting the consumer's forecasted weather conditions.

The campaign featured Meghan Trainor, the popular singer, songwriter, and influencer, in the style of a weathercast titled "The Radiance Report," which forecasted an approaching "e.l.f.ing glow storm."

The videos were served to women aged 18–48, e.l.f.'s

target audience, on The Weather Channel app, before they viewed the video content.

The copy and images were presented to people in key designated marketing areas (DMAs) based on time and weather patterns, which were clear, cloudy, rainy, or wintery. The units appeared front and center in The Weather Company's integrated marquee, its proprietary solution, which embedded e.l.f.'s creative into the current hyperlocal forecast on the app's home screen.

The campaign was delivered via The Weather Channel app and its digital out-of-home (DOOH) inventory in December 2022. Weather Targeting for DOOH via Vistar Media extended the weather-specific copy across DOOH screens.

Consumers in key markets saw e.l.f.'s messages during their daily routines through these placements based on current weather conditions in those respective locations. These DOOH screens appeared in pharmacies, outdoor panels, taxi or rideshare vehicles, grocery stores, malls, and more.

Results

The campaign experienced a 9.2 percent lift in brand awareness among women aged 25–34, a 17.3 percent increase in purchase intent, and an 8.9 percent higher lift in brand consideration compared to industry benchmarks.

e.l.f. used The Weather Company's weather data to help them reach the right person at the right time with the right message related to weather insights. e.l.f's ability to see outside of the box and use a third-party provider to harness a trove of data related to one of the most powerful consumer behavior signals resulted in the right outcome being achieved! It also resulted in e.l.f. gaining market share from their competition who weren't as innovative as e.l.f. by building engagement and offering utility to their most sought after consumers at a time when they'd be most in need of their personal care and beauty products.

DATA-DRIVEN PERSONALIZATION AND CUSTOMER ENGAGEMENT

Shelley E. Kohan, a digital and AI marketing and retail pundit and professor, shares that "Customer data platforms and insights are essential for personalizing and humanizing customer engagement. By analyzing vast amounts of data, AI helps marketers understand customer journeys better and tailor their approaches accordingly. The industry has moved from segmentation to micro-segmentation at scale."

Kohan adds that, "nearly half of the marketing leaders

see customer data collection and analytics as critical for enhancing engagement, according to a recent CMO Intentions study. Sophisticated chatbots and virtual assistants can interact in real time with customers, providing a highly personalized experience. GenAI uses personalized product and service recommendations to cater to individual customers, driving high engagement and deeper loyalty resulting in exceptionally tailored experiences in the shopper journey."

THE FUTURE IS AGENTIC AI

As artificial intelligence (AI) models rapidly evolve, the future will be what experts are calling agentic AI, or autonomous AI. This is a type of artificial intelligence that runs independently to design, execute, and optimize outputs.

Kohan shares that "Agentic AI will transform how companies are interacting with their customers and has the ability to drive deep customer engagement at scale. Agentic AI is a type of artificial intelligence that acts and responds in a humanistic way without human intervention. Imagine AI that understands context and can adapt responses based on understanding natural language. Humanistic AI. Ultimately, it acts like a personal assistant."

AI CHATBOTS DIFFER FROM AGENTIC AI

So, how will agentic AI differ from an AI chatbot? Kohan shares that "a chatbot gives programmed answers without much context and can ask basic questions. Where is my order? What was the shipping charge? When is the next sale? The exchange between customers and chatbots can become a pain point pretty quickly when the chatbot cannot understand a customer inquiry by asking for the customer to restate the question or ask the question in a different way (my favorite response). Or a constant surge of texting back and forth."

The biggest benefit to agentic AI is that it understands context and can act as a personal assistant or stylist. Kohan states, "I can say to an AI agent, please find me a dress for that party next week in Chicago. The response may include the weather in Chicago and also ask me if the event is formal, or outdoors. I can also say that I would like to see brown dresses with short sleeves and a zipper back. The agent comes back with choices for me to approve and with that I can ask that the dress be purchased and sent to my home address. And if I have been using this agent over time, it may remind me that I like the colors blue and red which is the theme of the event and include those dresses as well. Or throw in a matching pink scarf for the brown dress!"

To succeed with AI in marketing, brands need to do more than just basic audience targeting. They should focus on understanding each customer's journey and personalizing their approach. This isn't about making audience groups more detailed—it's about tailoring every interaction to feel unique to the individual. AI can process huge amounts of customer data and customize messages on a personal level. But marketers still need to use their own insights to be successful.

By leveraging data and AI as seen in the e.l.f. example, marketers can enhance their strategies, create more impactful campaigns, and achieve better outcomes in a highly competitive landscape.

With marketing communications becoming more complex and storytelling playing a key role in brand differentiation, ensuring content is consistent, high-quality, and on-brand is more important than ever.

Magid, a strategic consumer intelligence firm, recently launched an AI-powered intelligence product called Collaborator that generates customized marketing and sales content. Drawing from consumer data, proprietary insights, and industry best practices, this product creates messaging that's consistent, effective, and aligned with a brand's voice. Businesses can leverage it to scale content production across marketing, sales, and corporate communications—while maintaining brand integrity.

This innovative tool exemplifies how AI-driven technologies are transforming the way organizations communicate, making messaging more efficient and impactful.

Data and AI are revolutionizing marketing by enabling marketers to be more precise with their segmentation and personalization resulting in optimized efficiency. Here are a few key ways they are optimizing marketing effectiveness:

1. Customer Segmentation:
   - Data Analysis: AI algorithms analyze vast amounts of data to identify distinct customer segments based on behavior, demographics, and preferences.
   - Predictive Analytics: AI predicts future behaviors, allowing marketers to target potential high-value customers.
2. Personalization:
   - Dynamic Content: AI tailors content to individual preferences in real time, enhancing user engagement.

- Recommendation Engines: AI-driven systems recommend products and services based on past behavior and preferences data.

3. Enhanced Customer Experience:
   - Chatbots and Virtual Assistants: AI-powered chatbots provide instant customer support, improving satisfaction and retention.
   - Sentiment Analysis: AI monitors social media and feedback to gauge customer sentiment and adjust strategies accordingly.

AI ADOPTION AND APPROACH

CMOs play a pivotal role in driving the adoption of AI within their organizations. The first step in this journey is to identify specific-use cases where AI can significantly enhance both efficiency and user experience. In a recent interview with Director of Product Go-to-Market at Microsoft Vera Hsu, she highlighted the critical importance of establishing well-defined AI strategies that prioritize both people and processes. Hsu emphasized, "We need a human-centric approach." This means that marketers should focus on deploying AI strategies that not only solve existing problems but also unlock new opportunities for growth. By leveraging generative AI, marketers can create innovative solutions that drive business success. However, Hsu also pointed out that the rapid evolution of technology necessitates the continuous refinement of these strategies.

Ultimately, the success of AI adoption is deeply dependent on the ability of humans to effectively adapt to and integrate these technological advancements into their daily workflows. This means that beyond just implementing AI tools, there needs to be a focus on how these tools are used by people. It involves training and upskilling employees to ensure they are comfortable and proficient with the new technology. Additionally, it requires a cultural shift within organizations to embrace change and innovation.

HUMAN ELEMENT AND UPSKILLING ARE KEY TO IMPLEMENTING EFFECTIVE AI-INCORPORATED MARKETING CAMPAIGNS

"In essence, the human element is critical; it's about fostering an environment where people are not only equipped with the necessary skills but are also motivated to leverage AI to its fullest potential. This holistic approach ensures that AI becomes a seamless part of the workflow, driving efficiency and innovation," says Hsu.

MARKETERS NEED TO BE CAUTIOUS
OF AUTHENTICITY AND PRIVACY ISSUES

Marketers need to also be cautious of authenticity and privacy issues associated with hyperpersonalized marketing and brands should walk a fine line when it comes to this type of marketing. While personalization can create more relevant experiences, there's a point where it stops feeling helpful and starts feeling downright creepy. When ads seem *too* spot-on—like a brand predicting what you want before you even search for it—it can trigger unease rather than engagement. There's a psychological tipping point where consumers shift from feeling understood to feeling watched.

Take the common experience of discussing something in real life—maybe near a phone or smart device—only to see an ad for it online *before* ever searching for it. Whether or not our devices are actively listening, this phenomenon has fueled widespread discussions about privacy and digital surveillance. As a society, we've accepted that our online behavior is tracked, but there's an increasing awareness (and discomfort) around how much of our spoken word might be feeding into the algorithm.

The real challenge for brands is finding the right balance between relevance and privacy. AI-driven personalization should feel like a helpful assistant, not an intrusive eavesdropper. Instead of relying on tactics that make consumers feel monitored, brands should prioritize transparent, opt-in personalization—giving people control over their data, much like the recent privacy changes we've seen on social media. Ultimately, AI should enhance the customer experience, not manipulate it.

DATA IS ONLY AS GOOD AS THE INSIGHTS GAINED

Data collection can often be overwhelming so it's important to set up the right process. I first recommend for marketers to clearly define their objective(s) and audience. Next, assemble a talented team to collaborate and drive the process. Understanding and using the right data platforms, whether you're building your own in-house or collaborating with outside vendors, will help you implement the right inputs and systems to inform and optimize your data output. This step sets up your team to interpret and analyze the treasure trove of data in an organized and optimal fashion, paving the way for developing the right insights.

The data is only as good as the insights. The insights gained lead to ideation and problem-solving and lead marketers to do what they know best—creating a comprehensive strategy. Whether creating content, developing an ad, building a website, or designing an in-person event, the insights will drive the identification of your most sought-after customer base, making them the focal point of your entire campaign. Returning to that clearly defined objective and audience segment, marketers will have the data and insights to articulate, implement, and amplify an effective campaign. As Hsu shared, these rich data insights and outputs can only happen through a holistic, AI-implemented approach where the human element and AI upskilling deliver positive results.

Here are some tips on how AI and data can help you reach the right person with the right message in the right media environments at the right time:

1. Audience Targeting & Segmentation
   - **AI-Powered Customer Insights:** Machine learning can help analyze consumer data and segment audiences based on behavior, demographics, and preferences.
   - **Predictive Analytics:** AI can forecast purchasing behavior and identify high-value prospects.
   - **Look-Alike Audiences:** AI finds new prospects similar to existing high-value customers.
2. Personalization at Scale

- **Dynamic Content Optimization:** AI customizes messages based on user interactions.
- **Chatbots & Virtual Assistants:** AI-driven bots provide real-time, personalized recommendations.
- **Recommendation Engines:** AI suggests relevant products or content based on past behavior.

3. Right Media Environment Selection

- **Omnichannel Strategy:** AI helps ensure a seamless and consistent experience across multiple channels.
- **Sentiment Analysis:** AI analyzes social conversations to determine the best platforms for brand messaging.

4. Right Timing with Real-Time Data

- **Predictive Timing:** AI identifies the best moments to engage users.
- **Trigger-Based Marketing:** Automate messages based on real-time customer actions (e.g., cart abandonment).
- **Contextual Targeting:** AI uses location, weather, and time of day to enhance message relevance.

5. Marketing Automation & Performance Optimization
   - **A/B Testing at Scale:** AI tests different ad creatives, messages, and formats for optimization.
   - **Attribution Modeling:** AI tracks customer journeys to determine the most effective marketing channels.
   - **Budget Allocation Optimization:** AI dynamically shifts ad spend to top-performing channels.
6. Conversational & Voice Search Marketing
   - **AI Chatbots:** Engage customers through AI-powered chat interactions.
   - **Voice Search Optimization:** AI helps optimize content for voice-based search queries.
7. Ethical AI & Privacy-First Marketing
   - **Privacy-Centric AI Solutions**: AI ensures compliance with GDPR, CCPA, and other regulations.
   - **First-Party Data Utilization:** AI leverages predictive analytics to maximize first-party data in a cookieless future.

By integrating AI and data-driven strategies, you can enhance precision in targeting, personalization, media selection, and timing—ultimately boosting engagement and conversions.

3

Reaching the Right Person

Niche marketing and segmentation is so important when you're working with a small budget and trying to target a specific audience. Segmentation provides your marketing budget with efficiency. By prioritizing your audience segments, your marketing budget will go further while minimizing waste. Segmentation also allows you to fully immerse your team into the mindset and culture of

your targeted customer so that your messaging achieves optimal engagement.

I do a segmentation improvisation exercise in my class to demonstrate how thinking outside of the box when looking at primary and secondary target segments can make your marketing campaign more effective. Let's try this together.

Imagine you're coming out with new snowblower to sell. It's top of the line, high-performance snowblower with all the bells and whistles.

Think about who your most important customer is. Where do they live? Are they male or female? How old are they? How wealthy are they? The most common answers are someone living in a cold climate who are middle-aged, skewing to male who are in the upper- to middle-class income range. However, this past year I've had more responses to target females as well.

Now think about the mindset of the person. Describe someone you know who owned or currently owns a snowblower. For me it's one of my former neighbors who loved to rev up his snowblower at the first snowfall and make sure everyone knew he had the best snowblower in the neighborhood—perhaps in the state—it was very loud! Who else, besides someone who is somewhat "macho" is common among the type of person who owns a snowblower? For this top-of-the-line snowblower, this person is likely to be an "early adopter" who likes to have the latest and greatest toys. This person is also likely to be a "do-it-your-selfer." Otherwise, they'd likely pay to have someone come and plow their driveway and shovel their sidewalks. Let's take this further, have you heard the term "gadget-head"? This is someone who likes having items that they work on and fix and likes to get their hands dirty. The psychographic mindset of your potential customer is so important to describe and is sometimes the hardest piece to get data on and can often make or break a campaign.

Now that we have our primary target consumer pinned down, what are some secondary target segments?

Think about volume sales. Who would be likely to buy multiple snowblowers from you? How about landscapers, municipalities, schools, apartment management companies, etc.? These customers might be fewer in number but will purchase multiple snowblowers from you. You can never underestimate the 80/20 law that states that 80 percent of a company's sales usually comes from 20 percent of their customers. Segmentation enables you to laser in on this important segment by providing more nurturing attention and customer service to assure that they are always happy and have your brand at the top of their mind at all times.

Many businesses find themselves spending significant resources on marketing efforts that don't successfully reach the right audience. The result? Wasted budget, low conversion rates, and frustration.

This custom-tailored audience segmentation can help you focus your marketing efforts on the existing and potential customers most likely to convert, ensuring your message reaches the right people at the right time. This allows you to communicate directly with the people genuinely interested in what you have to say, rather than shouting from the rooftops and hoping the right person hears you.

Targeting the right person is crucial. If you don't know who your audience truly is, there are a variety of ways that you can find out. If you have customer relationship marketing (CRM) or any customer data—use this information to your advantage to uncover trends in customer demographics and psychographics. You can also conduct surveys and interviews to learn more and ensure you're not making assumptions about who your target audience really is.

National retailers like CVS, Target, Staples, REI, and Best Buy use post-purchase surveys to gauge customer satisfaction with their online, in-app, and in-store shopping experiences.

These surveys typically include questions such as:

- How would you rate your shopping experience on a scale of 1–10?
- Did you find everything you needed during your visit?
- If a shopper initiated a return, they might be asked: How was your in-store return experience? Was it easy?

By collecting this feedback, retailers gain valuable insights into their customer base—distinguishing loyal shoppers from occasional visitors and refining their shopping experience to better meet customer needs.

Target marketing is any marketing activity aimed at specific customer segments. There are many ways you can identify and target the right consumers for your brand. For example, you can use Google Ads targeted marketing as part of your search engine optimization (SEO) strategy to reach your intended audience based on their demographics, interests, online behaviors, and more. So if you're a surf shop, you can purchase keywords related to consumers who are likely to be surfers so that when these words are typed into a google query, your website's ad appears. Some obvious surf shop related keywords might be: waves, surfboards, wetsuit, wax. You could also purchase keywords that indicate a related interest in surfing such as skateboards, the Beach Boys, and California. At the same time, you can use email marketing to deliver personalized content directly to your customers' inboxes based on purchase history, location, engagement level, and other relevant factors.

Your target audience is the specific group of individuals you want to reach with your marketing initiatives. It's important to identify your target audience so your brand can reach the right people with the right message. Digging into the details to get a clear picture of your primary audience can make a big impact on your brand.

Once you've identified who you are trying to reach, research where those people are, where they consume media, and what times of the day they're most likely to engage with your content so that you can target them most effectively.

People who own boats are likely to be dog owners

Let's imagine that you are launching an innovative dog products website. How can you identify people who are most likely to be dog lovers? Did you know that research shows that people who own boats are likely to love dogs? Did you also know that 80 percent of dog product purchases are within the first year of a dog's life? What is one of the first items that a dog owner purchases that is an indicator that they care about their dog and have money to invest in their puppy's well-being? Dog pet insurance! In fact, there are lists of owners of dog pet insurance that you can purchase. You can even purchase a first-year owner of dog insurance list. This filtered list will ensure that you're targeting first-year dog owners who are likely to have expendable income and may need to purchase your premium, innovative dog products. Let's go!

This type of smart, audience detective work

and research will set you apart in winning market share and sales! (This is the same type of audience analysis Harry's did in their early days to overcome Gillette).

To maximize impact, you need to hypertarget your ideal customer using advanced segmentation and psychographics—going beyond demographics to understand motivations, interests, and behaviors. Here are some recommendations for reaching the optimal person:

1. Utilize Psychographic Marketing for Deeper Insights
   - Identify the lifestyle choices, values, personality traits, and interests of your ideal customer.
   - Create audience personas based on their aspirations, pain points, and buying motivations.
   - Align your messaging with their emotional triggers (e.g., adventure for thrill-seekers, security for cautious buyers).
2. Leverage Hypertargeting & Microsegmentation
   - Use data-driven insights to refine audience segments (e.g., young professionals who love fitness vs. stay-at-home parents who prioritize convenience).

- Segment by buying behavior (e.g., repeat customers vs. onetime buyers).
- Combine demographic, geographic, and psychographic data to create ultra-niche marketing campaigns.

3. Go Beyond Basic, Data-Driven Marketing
   - Use behavioral tracking to predict customer needs before they arise (e.g., fitness gear for marathon trainers).
   - Leverage AI and machine learning to refine targeting based on real-time engagement.
   - Implement predictive analytics to anticipate what customers will want next.

4. A/B Test and Optimize Continuously
   - Test different audience segments.
   - Use real-time analytics to adjust targeting and creative strategies.
   - Measure engagement, conversions, and customer feedback to refine future campaigns.

By combining hypertargeting, psychographics, and niche marketing, you can reach the right person.

4

Right Message

Message is King

T he Holy Grail of Marketing lies in reaching the right person with the right message in the right environment at the right time to deliver the right outcome. The right message, paramount among these factors, is the bridge between a brand and its audience—a conversation that happens when the brand isn't in the room.

UNDERSTANDING THE "WHY" IN MARKETING:
WHY THE MESSAGE IS KING

Before developing a strategy, marketers must understand the consumer's behaviors, ambitions, and pain points without making assumptions. This understanding comes from listening, observing, and empathizing. Effective messaging meets customers where they are and resonates with their needs, desires, and emotions. In marketing, the message is king—its power determines what consumers hear and how they feel, remember, and act. This principle holds true across industries and understanding the "why" behind consumer behavior is the foundation for crafting impactful messaging.

For brands to truly connect with the right audience, their messaging must be intentional and deeply rooted in understanding. This requires more than just knowing basic demographics—it demands a deep dive into psychographics.

Brands need to go beyond surface-level data and understand their consumers' behaviors, ambitions, personality traits, and pain points—without making assumptions. True connection comes from recognizing the audience's unique situations and empathizing with their experiences.

Today, AI tools provide vast amounts of data—the "what," "who," "how many," and "how often"—but they rarely uncover the "why." Without the "why," campaigns can lack the emotional resonance needed to connect. To find the "why," marketers must embrace the customer's perspective, making them the experts on their experience.

As technology continues to commoditize language and as AI starts to level the playing field, James Wright, executive director at Interbrand, a leading global brand consultancy firm, states that "purpose within a message will increasingly drive deeper engagement while also elevating their customer lifetime value (CLV). The absence of which will result in a brand becoming another commodity in a consumer's life who will buy you and build a transactional relationship." We'll cover the importance of brand purpose in more depth in Chapter 7.

THE POWER OF CONTEXTUAL RELEVANCE

A message only thrives when it fits the context in which it's received. Contextually relevant messaging is a profound component that can transform impact; it's when messaging is crafted and delivered to a consumer in the proper context, providing deliberate relevance; it ensures that the person receives a message tailored to their personalized needs, desires, or interests exactly when they're most likely to engage with it.

For example, brands that acknowledged uncertainty and offered practical support during the COVID-19 pandemic saw stronger connections with their audiences. It wasn't just the mediums they chose, but the message itself—empathetic, reassuring, and timely—that resonated.

BLUE DIAMOND ALMONDS—EMOTIONS

Take, for example, Blue Diamond Almonds, an almond brand positioned as a premium gift item for holidays and special occasions. The company wanted to shift perceptions, making its product an everyday snack, so it developed an animated commercial featuring women gaining energy from almonds in order to better play with their kids. However, a quantitative research firm declared the ads ineffective, citing too many vignettes and insufficient product focus.

"The quantitative data missed the emotional response of the audience. Qualitative research revealed the genuine issue: the women in the ads were portrayed as too thin and attractive, making the target audience feel judged and alienated. The strategy of promoting almonds as an everyday snack was solid, but the message failed to empathize with the audience," explained Founder and President of Prosperity Productions, Inc. Lori Hamilton.

REACHING A NICHE AUDIENCE
WITH THE RIGHT MESSAGE

Imagine you're the head of marketing for a private jet company who is targeting a niche audience of centimillionaires. These are people worth $100 million and who can spend $200,000 to $1,000,000 per year on private jet travel, including hourly contracts, fractional or full ownership of a jet. There are approximately 20,000 private jet owners in the world and 100,000 people who fly privately annually. Although defining this audience may appear easy, reaching them with the right message can be a challenge. Unless you're Matteo Atti, global CMO at one of the world's largest and most reputable business and private aviation providers, VistaJet.

ADAPT YOUR MESSAGE CONTEXTUALLY
TO THEIR NEED AND DESIRED OUTCOME

Matteo shares that in general, the private jet traveler is a highly successful person, so the best thing to do as a marketer is to respect their lack of time and the fact that everyone is trying to reach them. The biggest opportunity to engage with this highly select audience is to communicate a desirable experience. You need to adapt your message contextually to their needs and desired outcome. This is crucial. Instead of having one message for all channels and segments, you need to focus on showing the personality of your brand, how much effort you put into things, how much detail you're able to manage, how you're able to transform the meaning of generic time into personal time. When you are working in digital, the time frame that you're applying is about speed. It is all about *I need to solve a problem.* At a private jet terminal, also known as an fixed-based operator (FBO), advertisements will focus on on-time scheduling, because anyone standing around an FBO is usually waiting for their aircraft, providing you with the opportunity to say, *Would you like to give us a try? VistaJet will provide you with a better experience.*

Choosing the right message is essential and often the environment becomes part of the message. Equally important is the clarity and relevance of the content. Let's take a look at these examples:

1. Associate your brand with the outcome and benefit it delivers to the consumer: Sharpie, a foremost brand of creative markers, uses a marketing strategy that goes beyond selling

their markers directly. Instead, it celebrates its users' creative works. The brand aligns itself with artistic expression by showcasing drawings and projects made with Sharpie products. This approach creates a halo effect: consumers associate Sharpie with creativity and individuality without being told to buy a pen. Sharpie's influencer program, which supports superfans hosting creative events, reinforces this ethos by empowering users rather than dictating the narrative.

2. Focus on your thought leadership while providing utility for your targeted audience: Asset managers and insight-sharing asset managers who often deal with long sales cycles succeed by sharing valuable insights in environments where their target audience is already seeking knowledge. For example, a conference talk on market volatility positions the speaker as an expert and fosters trust. The audience perceives the presenter as insightful and approachable, creating a positive association with the brand without overtly pushing a product.

3. Augment your message using the latest technologies: Imagine walking past a clothing store

like Michael Kors while holding your phone. A targeted video showcasing the brand's latest collection appears, drawing you into the store. This example demonstrates how blending digital engagement with real-world behavior can create a seamless and compelling brand experience.

As the Canadian communications theorist Marshall McLuhan famously said, "The medium is the message," but only when the message itself is compelling does it make an impact.

HOW DOES A COMPANY EMBODY ITS BRAND MESSAGE?

How does a company embody its brand message? Look no further than Apple. Steve Jobs envisioned Apple as a brand that transcended mere technology. He wanted Apple to be a symbol of creativity, simplicity, and innovation. He wanted Apple to be a brand that emotionally resonated with people and became an integral part of their daily lives. His marketing strategy reflected this vision, focusing on simplicity, creativity, and building a deeper connection with consumers.

Under Jobs's leadership, Apple was more than just a

consumer electronics company—it was a movement that challenged the way people thought about technology.

Apple universally embodies its brand message. Its marketing message is unique due to its consistent focus on simplicity, emotional connection, innovation, and premium positioning.

Here are a few key aspects of Apple's successful marketing strategy:

Lifestyle-Oriented: Rather than focusing solely on product features, Apple's marketing portrays their products as essential for a modern, creative, and high-performing lifestyle. This positions Apple as a brand that understands its users and enhances their daily lives.

Simplicity and Clarity: Apple's marketing is known for its clean, minimalist approach. Their messaging is direct and easy to understand. Apple's ads often focus on a single idea or product feature, making it easy for customers to easily grasp Apple's value.

Emotional Appeal: Apple's marketing emphasizes how their products enhance the user's life, focusing on the emotional connection rather than just the technical specs. Apple aims to create a sense of belonging, creativity, and empowerment, positioning their products as more than just tools.

__Innovation and Design:__ Apple markets itself as a leader in innovation and design. They emphasize their products' sleek aesthetics and cutting-edge technology, creating the perception that their products are ahead of the curve, setting trends rather than following them.

NIKE'S AUTHENTIC COMMITMENT TO GENDER EQUALITY IN SPORTS

Nike's decision to spotlight women athletes aligns with the rapid growth of the media coverage of women's sports, which has increased from just 3 to 5.5 percent historically to 15 percent of all sports coverage in 2022. If this trend continues, women's sports are projected to make up 20 percent of all sports coverage by 2025—a shift that reinforces Nike's positioning as a champion of gender equality in sports.

This strategy not only appeals to female athletes but also resonates with socially conscious consumers who value brands with authentic commitments to diversity and inclusion. The momentum is evident: sponsorships in women's sports have grown 20 percent year-over-year, and female athletes are securing 18 percent more brand partnerships than in previous years.

Additionally, the WNBA recently became the first women's league to reach a billion-dollar valuation, a clear sign that investment and audience engagement in women's sports are surging. By capitalizing on this movement, Nike strengthens its market position while fostering deeper connections with a rapidly growing and highly engaged audience.

STORYTELLING IS THE HEARTBEAT OF GREAT MARKETING AS SHOWN BY A+E GLOBAL MEDIA

"In today's fast-moving, fragmented media world, one thing still holds true: storytelling is the heartbeat of great marketing," says David DeSocio, EVP Ad Sales Marketing and Partnership at A+E Global Media. "However, it's no longer just about telling a story—it's about telling the right story, in the right way, on the right platforms."

At A+E Global Media, they've seen how storytelling has evolved from traditional sponsorships and product placements into fully immersive, cross-platform experiences. Brand content now lives everywhere—on TV, on phones, in social feeds, and in streaming queues. And the brands that get it right? They're not just inserting themselves—they're creating content with which people actually want to engage. The company has always embraced a forward-facing, technology first approach, marrying it's best-in-class content with creative, data-driven advertiser solutions that drive results. It all starts by understanding the brand's goals. Whether it's building awareness, sparking engagement, or driving direct sales, every move needs to tie back to where the brand is in the consumer journey/marketing funnel. Strategy and execution must be aligned, from the first brainstorm to execution.

If you look at the history of media, storytelling has always changed and followed technology. The disciplines have evolved together—with new technologies enabling new kinds of stories and connections. Print media gave us long-form copy. Radio brought in voice and emotion. TV let us show instead of just tell. The internet and artificial intelligence? Those have blown the doors wide open. Now, content needs to have a strategic life across all platforms because audiences are everywhere, allowing for not just hyper-targeting, but true customization of a brand's story so it can be told and experienced in new and deeper ways.

Consumers today spend multiple hours a day with media, often jumping across platforms and devices. That's a challenge, but it's also an opportunity. When brands meet audiences where they are, with stories that speak to them, amazing things happen. Culled from recent media reports, a few examples of A+E Global Media's success in building impactful brand content partnerships include:

KFC and Lifetime's branded content piece, "A Recipe for Seduction"—a 15-minute, tongue-in-cheek romance and murder mystery featuring Mario Lopez as a dreamy Colonel Sanders. It sounds wild—and it was. However, it worked and generated double-digit increases in KPIs and billions of impressions within just four days.[*]

Or look at *The New Lincolns*, a moving collaboration between Ancestry.com and The HISTORY Channel. The series uncovered the stories of African Americans connected to Abraham Lincoln's legacy. It resonated so deeply many viewers didn't even realize it was branded content. That's the kind of seamless integration brands dream about.[†]

Even legendary brands are looking for new ways to connect. Campbell's Soup found a new touchpoint with "A Spoonful of Joy," a holiday spot featuring an autistic child and his mother. It wasn't just inclusive—it was deeply

---

[*] "Colonel Sanders' Next KFC Commercial Is Also a Steamy Lifetime Drama," *Variety*, December 7, 2020.

[†] "History Channel Plans Short Mini-Series Backed by Ancestry to Accompany 'Lincoln' Documentary," *Variety*, February 16, 2020.

human. In fact, leaning in to authenticity, this beautiful story was inspired by the real-life experience of a Lifetime creative executive.*

"These stories work because they're authentic. They're relevant. And they're told with purpose," DeSocio adds. "It's not just about being seen—it's about being felt." That's the core of A+E Global Media's "multiplatform advantage." Campaigns that run across multiple platforms consistently outperform single-channel efforts, driving double-digit lifts in awareness, likability, and purchase intent. DeSocio says, "It's not enough to just be on those platforms. You want to do things that are interesting and unique to those platforms. This customization enables our partners to cut through the clutter and create engagement that is immediate, buzzworthy, and measurable."

DeSocio shares that "at the end of the day, effective branded storytelling comes down to orchestration. It's a mix of creativity, data, strategy, and heart. Marketers who get it right don't just sell a product or service—they build a connection that leaves a lasting impression on consumers. And that's what turns campaigns into movements."

---

* "Campbell's holiday ad inspired by the real mother-son story of an A+E Networks executive," *Ad Age*, December 13, 2020.

"Brands that lead with their values, communicate with empathy, and meet consumers where they are—those are the ones that truly stand out."

As David DeSocio puts it, "It's hard to go wrong if you listen to and follow your consumer. That's where you make the connection. The content plays a part, the environment plays a part, and the brand benefits play a part. But in the end, it starts and ends with the consumer. Did you tell a story that was authentic and worth their time and attention? If you did, the results are sure to follow."

It's not just about being loud—it's about being real. When your message aligns with what your audience cares about, and when it's delivered with heart and purpose, that's when the magic happens.

GROWING POWER OF MINORITY CONSUMERS

The rapid growth of minority consumer groups—Hispanic, Black, and Asian—presents a major opportunity for marketers:

- Over the past decade, the white population declined for the first time in history (-2.6 percent), while Black, multiracial, Hispanic, and Asian populations drove overall US growth.

- By 2045, non-Hispanic whites will make up less than half of the US population.
- The buying power of minority groups is surging—from $4.2 trillion in 2020 to a projected $7 trillion by 2025.
- Multicultural consumers are younger than their non-Hispanic white counterparts: Hispanics have a median age of thirty; Blacks thirty-five; Asian-Americans thirty-eight; compared to forty-four for non-Hispanic whites.

While inclusive marketing is important from a diversity perspective, these statistics highlight an undeniable business case—it's not just the right thing to do, it's the smart thing to do.

REACHING AN AUDIENCE IN-LANGUAGE AND IN-CULTURE IS OF VITAL IMPORTANCE

Reaching an audience *"in-language and in-culture"* means crafting messages that are not only linguistically accurate but also culturally relevant—ensuring true resonance with your intended audience.

Culture plays a crucial role in how people interpret messages. Every audience brings its own values, beliefs, and norms to the table. By understanding these cultural backgrounds, you can avoid missteps and ensure your message is received as intended.

Language barriers and cultural nuances can complicate communication, but the key is to simplify without losing meaning. When in doubt, prioritize clarity—using plain, accessible language that connects with your audience while staying true to their cultural context.

When I was vice president of client development at Univision—one of the largest Hispanic TV and cable broadcast companies—I worked with major US brands to help them tap into the fastest-growing consumer segment: Hispanics, who today make up a third of the US population.

One of my key targets was LG Electronics. At the time, LG had never invested in Hispanic media, while its main competitor, Samsung, was actively advertising on Univision and seeing significant success. My challenge was to demonstrate to LG that every day they weren't running Spanish-language ads, they were losing millions in TV sales to their competitor.

Winning LG over took months of strategic meetings. Our first session included Univision's consumer insights team, where we educated LG on the power of the Hispanic consumer. We emphasized how, in Hispanic households, the television is the central gathering place, where families watch soccer and telenovelas together. We also guided LG on how to adapt its English-language ads into culturally relevant Spanish-language campaigns that would truly resonate with Univision's audience.

Ultimately, we convinced LG to launch a test campaign in key Hispanic markets—Miami, Chicago, and New York. The results spoke for themselves. After seeing great success, LG expanded into a national, multimillion-dollar advertiser with Univision.

Technology has made it easier than ever to connect with your audience. Platforms like Facebook, Instagram, and LinkedIn offer powerful tools including language translation to engage with customers globally, keeping your brand top of mind and driving higher engagement.

But it doesn't stop there—leveraging videos, infographics, and interactive content can capture attention and improve message retention. Modern technology provides endless opportunities for marketers to communicate creatively and effectively to a multicultural audience.

FIVE COMMANDMENTS FOR
SUCCESSFUL BRANDING

Former North America Chairwomen of LVMH (Louis Vuitton Moët Hennessy) Pauline Brown has spent decades shaping luxury brands. Brown coined the term "aesthetic intelligence" and defines it as the ability to "understand, interpret and leverage sensory and emotional experiences to create powerful, memorable brands. It's not just about creating beauty—it's about creating a multisensory experience that makes a brand irresistible." This means going beyond functionality and engaging with the senses and emotions. "It's not just about selling a product, it's about crafting an experience," Brown emphasizes. This is why brands such as Apple, Rolex, and Prada transcend product utility to create immersive experiences that engage the narrating self (emotional, sensory) making these brands enduring and aspirational.

Brown shares five key components that brands should cultivate to enhance their aesthetic intelligence:

1. **Sensitivity:** Recognizing and appreciating beauty in various forms.
2. **Interpretation:** Understanding the emotional and psychological impact of design.
3. **Curation:** Selecting and refining elements that align with the brand's identity.
4. **Articulation:** Expressing a brand's unique aesthetic in a compelling way.
5. **Empathy:** Understanding and responding to the emotions and needs of consumers.

ABRAHAM MASLOW'S HIERARCHY OF NEEDS

Maslow's hierarchy of needs is a psychological theory that categorizes human needs from basic to advanced:

- **Physiological:** Basic survival needs such as food, water, shelter, and rest.
- **Safety:** The need for security, stability, and protection from harm.
- **Love & Belonging:** Emotional needs for friendship, intimacy, and social connection.
- **Esteem:** The desire for respect, recognition, and a sense of achievement.
- **Self-Actualization:** The drive to reach one's full potential, including personal growth and creativity.

This theory is often illustrated as a pyramid, with fundamental needs at the base and higher-level aspirations at the top. Maslow suggested that individuals are generally motivated to fulfill these needs in order, progressing upward as each level is met.

Key Insights on Maslow's Theory:

SELF-ACTUALIZA-TION
morality, creativity,
spontaneity, acceptance,
experience purpose, meaning
and inner potential

SELF-ESTEEM
confidence, achievement, respect of others,
the need to be a unique individual

LOVE AND BELONGING
friendship, family, intimacy, sense of connection

SAFETY AND SECURITY
health, employment, property, family and social abilty

PHYSIOLOGICAL NEEDS
breathing, food, water, shelter, clothing, sleep

- Progression Isn't Always Linear—People may move back and forth between levels based on life circumstances and external factors.
- A Humanistic Perspective—Maslow's approach emphasizes the whole person, focusing on overall well-being rather than isolated psychological symptoms.

MAKE YOUR MESSAGE THE CROWN JEWEL AND SUCCESS WILL FOLLOW

Remember that while data and tools provide essential tactical guidance, the timeless power of a great message will always set your brand apart. Make the message your crown jewel and success will follow.

FINAL THOUGHTS

Marketing is most effective when it's focused on customers' needs, desires, and context. A great message is like a dinner party guest who listens, engages, and adds value to the conversation, eliciting and connecting through empathy and understanding.

Marketers must connect with consumers on a human level through qualitative research, ethnography, or simply asking the right questions. By doing so, they can craft messages that resonate deeply and are delivered through mediums that enhance their relevance and impact by focusing on what truly matters to the target audience. This alignment between message, medium, and audience transforms marketing efforts into meaningful connections and lasting success.

Blending the components of the Holy Grail of Marketing may need adjusting to get this framework just right, but one truth is constant: the message is king. It is the foundation of connection, trust, and loyalty. As tools, trends, and technologies evolve, the brands that thrive prioritize crafting meaningful, emotionally resonant messages.

Brand Purpose

Why It's the Ultimate Differentiator

In today's world, where technology—particularly AI—has commoditized functional advantages and leveled the playing field, what truly sets brands apart? It's about winning the hearts and minds of consumers. And at the core lies brand purpose—the "why" behind a brand's existence in the lives of its customers.

Before embarking on any marketing initiative, a period of deep introspection is crucial. To achieve the right outcomes—reaching the right person with the right message in the right environment at the right time—marketers must first understand the core identity of their brand.

I had the opportunity to guest lecture recently at my alma mater, Rutgers University, addressing the capstone marketing class taught by a renowned marketing professor, Dr. Can Uslay.

I asked Dr. Uslay about the importance of brand purpose related to his studies and forthcoming book, *Navigating Brand Activism*. Dr. Uslay shared that "defining your ideal customer is paramount. Even brands with broad appeal, like Nike, recognize that their message won't resonate with everyone. Just as a health-conscious consumer might never be persuaded to visit Wendy's, no matter how healthy their new salad options, your brand must identify its natural audience. This understanding is intrinsically linked to your brand's purpose. However, unless you are starting from scratch, your brand also comes with baggage which you must acknowledge and work with, at least in the short- to medium-term."

A brand's heritage and possible baggage is important to explore and to address within your brand's message to current and new audiences that you're looking to attract. Dr. Uslay recommends the following questions that are important to ask at the onset of developing your marketing plan:

Scope: Is your brand global, like McDonald's, or regional, like In-N-Out Burger?

Specialization: Is it a generalist, like Walmart, or a specialist, like Ferrari? If the latter, is it a product specialist (WD-40), a market specialist (Etsy), or both (Bang & Olufsen)?

Stage of Development: Is it a fledgling brand, like Liquid Death, or one with a strong heritage, like Yuengling?

Brand Personality: What are the defining characteristics of your brand? Is it playful, serious, innovative, or traditional?

Brand Evolution: What stage is your brand at in its life cycle? Is it fighting for survival, or has it achieved a level of esteem and recognition?

Brand Reputation: Is your brand beloved, like Costco, or does it face challenges in consumer perception?

Answering these questions is fundamental to identifying not only your target audience but also the authentic message that will resonate with them. Dr. Uslay explains further that your business mission and experiences will inevitably shape your marketing beliefs and principles. These can be formalized into an internal marketing doctrine, providing a framework for all your brands.

BRAND MANIFESTO DEFINES WHAT YOUR BRAND STANDS FOR—NOT JUST A TAGLINE

The halo effect of what ultimately shapes your brand should be publicly formalized into your brand's manifesto. This is a powerful statement that defines what your brand stands for—its mission, values, and purpose beyond just selling products or services. It's not just a tagline or a marketing slogan; it's a deeper expression of why your brand exists and the impact you want to make.

Your brand manifesto is a statement of what you hope to achieve—it's a powerful way to set your brand apart and attract customers who truly connect with your values.

When people feel aligned with what you stand for, they're more likely to not just buy from you but also become enthusiastic supporters of your brand. We saw this come to life in my earlier Harry's case study. Harry's manifesto is what propelled it forward to take on the giant, Gillette.

MORE THAN A LIST OF NICE-SOUNDING GOALS

But here's the key: a manifesto isn't just a list of nice-sounding goals. It should be something real and actionable, shaping everything you do—from the products you create to the way you market them. It's a guiding force that keeps your brand focused and consistent, making it easier for both your team and your customers to understand what you're all about.

Dr. Uslay shares a great example and explains that "everyone knows Patagonia stands for sustainability; it is 'in the business of the planet' to protect nature. Its core values are Quality, Integrity, Environmentalism, Justice, and being Not Bound by Convention. It is not such a surprise then that it launched a Black Friday campaign that said, 'Don't Buy This Jacket' and sued the president of the United States to protect a national monument. Such activism would not have worked for any of the other brands I mentioned but fits Patagonia like a snug climbing glove."

Burt's Bees is a great example of a brand that sets itself apart through its social mission and brand manifesto. Founded in Maine in 1984 by Burt Shavitz and Roxanne Quimby, the brand has a unique origin story. Burt, an avid beekeeper, labeled his hives "Burt's Bees" to track them when thieves carried them off. One day, while driving his bright-yellow pickup truck, he picked up Roxanne, an artist hitchhiking on the roadside. The two quickly connected and began making lip balm and candles using beeswax from Burt's hives.

From the start, their brand manifesto was clear: *Since we take from nature, we must preserve it so that we can all live well.* This commitment is reflected in the brand's tagline: "By Nature. For Nature. For All."

Burt's Bees reinforces its mission through its website, stating: "Burt's Bees is an Earth-friendly, natural personal care company. We create natural, Earth-friendly personal care products formulated to help you maximize your well-being and that of the world around you." Its product lineup includes personal care essentials like hand and body butter, lip balms, body creams, and serums—all crafted with natural ingredients.

In 2007, Burt's Bees was acquired by The Clorox Company for $925 million. At the time, Beth Singer, Clorox's executive vice president of strategy and growth, emphasized the alignment between the two brands, stating: "Burt's Bees' mission, 'We make people's lives better every day—naturally,' is a terrific complement to Clorox's mission, 'We make everyday life better, every day.' "

Beyond its products, Burt's Bees maintains a strong commitment to sustainability. The brand uses recyclable packaging, educates consumers on recycling and home composting, and ensures sustainability across all materials.

Burt's Bees stands out in the crowded personal care and cosmetics market not only through its signature yellow packaging but also through its brand messaging. Visitors to its website quickly grasp its ethos with phrases like "Mindfully Made" and "Quality, transparency, kindness. That's our mantra." While many personal care brands focus solely on product benefits, Burt's Bees goes further—combining high-quality offerings with a mission-driven foundation that resonates with conscious consumers.

"Strong brands think beyond the first sale—they create narratives that span a customer's lifetime," said James Wright, executive director at Interbrand, a leading global brand consultancy.

A well-defined brand's purpose isn't just a catchy slogan or marketing gimmick—it's the intrinsic foundation of a brand's identity, a strategic asset that fuels growth, drives positive social impact, and builds rock-solid loyalty.

WHAT IS BRAND PURPOSE?

Simply put, purpose answers the fundamental question: *Why does this brand exist?* Purpose captures a brand's unique value and how it enriches customers' lives. Without a clear purpose, brands risk becoming just another commodity, stuck in transactional relationships lacking the emotional connection that leads to customers' brand champions and long-term loyalty. This loyalty transforms one-off purchases into lasting relationships, turning customers into brand advocates and even stakeholders in a shared journey.

Take TOMS, the shoe and accessory company, which activated its purpose by blending functional needs with a powerful desire for social good. The company's One for One® model gives away a pair of shoes for every pair sold—a program that resonates deeply. By donating one third of their profits through cash grants and partnerships with community organizations, TOMS transforms a simple purchase into an act of positive impact, bringing their "When you wear TOMS, you Wear Good" slogan to life and creating an emotional engagement that goes far beyond the product itself.

"TOMS has transformed its purpose into a promise—a promise that aligns with their customers' moral principles and values," Wright explains.

Even a giant like Walmart understands the power of

purpose. Their mission to "help people save money so they can live better" connects a tangible benefit (saving money) with a profound emotional outcome (improving one's life). By weaving this purpose into every customer touchpoint, from bottom-funnel tactics like promotions to overarching campaigns, Walmart is building meaningful relationships and positioning itself as an indispensable partner in its customers' lives.

SOCIAL IMPACT AND THE RISE
OF CONSCIOUS CONSUMERS

The social impact of a strong brand purpose is undeniable. By aligning with societal values, brands elevate their role in the world, inspiring loyalty, advocacy, and a sense of shared mission. Today's consumers, especially millennials and Gen Zs, actively seek out brands with a genuine purpose, contributing to causes they care about. In fact, a recent OnePoll study commissioned by TOMS found that a significant majority (80 percent) of these younger consumers are more likely to base their purchases on a brand's mission or purpose. On the flip side, they're also quick to boycott brands that contradict their values, with 74 percent saying they're likely to boycott brands for crossing an ethical line. Therefore, for brands looking to connect with these generations, genuine purpose and transparent communications are crucial for a competitive edge.

IMPORTANCE OF AUTHENTICITY

Here's the bottom line: brand purpose must be genuine. Consumers have a keen eye for inauthenticity and can easily see through marketing jargon. True brand purpose requires a deep understanding of customer needs and a real commitment to delivering value that resonates on both a functional and emotional level. When purpose is authentic, brands don't just exist in customers' lives; they become essential.

"Brand purpose is the heartbeat of a brand's identity, inspiring trust, loyalty, and action," Wright says. "It's built on moments of connection that resonate not by small transactional gains, but by the emotional bond it nurtures over time."

PRADA, SADIE SINK, AND THE
GUARDIANS OF THE OCEAN

Last night, while walking to meet a friend for dinner in SoHo, NYC, I was stopped in my tracks by a striking Prada billboard on West Broadway. It featured actress Sadie Sink, best known for her role in Netflix's *Stranger Things* (2017–present). See below picture I took.

The image captures Sink in La Paz, Mexico, where she stars in a National Geographic CreativeWorks miniseries about whale sharks, known as the "gardeners of the ocean." These essential creatures play a crucial role in marine ecosystems but face threats from overfishing. The billboard perfectly reflects Prada's brand purpose, displayed prominently in one of NYC's most stylish neighborhoods.

WHY ARE WHALE SHARKS SO IMPORTANT?

As the world's largest fish, whale sharks help regulate ocean health by feeding on plankton and algae, maintaining balance in the Pacific Ocean's ecosystem.

PRADA'S COMMITMENT TO
OCEAN CONSERVATION

Since 2019, Prada's SEA BEYOND educational program, in partnership with UNESCO's Intergovernmental Oceanographic Commission, has raised awareness about marine conservation worldwide.

- One percent of proceeds from the Prada Re-Nylon for SEA BEYOND Collection go toward ocean education initiatives.
- Episodes of the miniseries can be viewed at prada.com.
- More than 14,000 Prada employees have been trained in ocean literacy through virtual reality educational content.

This campaign is a powerful blend of fashion, education, and environmental activism, reinforcing how brands can leverage their platforms for meaningful impact.

A recent research study by Interbrand, in partnership with NewtonX and Brodeur Partners, reveals a strong link between a company's brand strength and its share price. The report, *How Brand Impacts Share Price*, examines the valuation of S&P 500 companies, investor perceptions of brand, and how businesses can achieve a more accurate share price valuation.

While companies naturally aim to increase their share price, the study found that few have optimized their brand communications to reflect an accurate price-to-earnings (P/E) evaluation. Insights from 241 investor relations professionals, analysts, and journalists across twenty-seven industries highlight a key issue: while the investment community recognizes the value of a strong brand, they often lack a deep understanding of its impact.

Interbrand's research uncovers the disconnect between share price and brand perception—and how companies can bridge this gap.

To strengthen brand understanding and drive share price growth, Interbrand recommends four key steps:

1. **Develop a Brand Valuation Model**
   Showing how brand strength, role of brand, and financial performance work together, a brand valuation model helps strengthen understanding of how well a brand is working to deliver shareholder returns.

2. **Conduct Financial Community Research**
   Develop a foundational understanding of how the investment community currently perceives your

brand. How aligned are these perceptions with the actual brand—and what differences are the most detrimental to your valuation?

3. **Analyze Communication Effectiveness**

   Conduct a review of your current investor relations and public relations plans to determine which of your touchpoints and assets need to be improved. This can range from incremental change to a true transformation.

4. **Revise Your Brand Strategy**

   Determine what isn't working for your brand in order to change perceptions, such as ensuring you have a *purpose* that guides action against a time-bound, measurable *ambition*. This will help build an understanding of what drives performance and where your brand has the potential for *iconic moves*. As the strategy evolves, the team will need to provide regular updates to continually shift perceptions in your brand's favor.

YOU CAN'T MANAGE WHAT YOU CAN'T MEASURE.

I recently came across a fascinating study on brand purpose and success by Zürn, Buder, and Unfried. It highlights how more companies today are embracing a purpose beyond profit—showing they care about social responsibility and sustainability. The challenge? There haven't been reliable ways to measure a brand's true purpose, and as the saying goes, *you can't manage what you can't measure.*

At its core, a business exists to provide products or services that benefit customers, which in turn helps the company meet financial goals. But how do consumers perceive a brand's purpose? That's where the Perceived Purpose Scale (see image below) comes in.

Instead of analyzing corporate reports, this study takes a consumer-driven approach, measuring how people perceive a brand's purpose through direct interactions. Researchers asked four hundred German consumers to rate the world's one hundred most valuable brands (per Interbrand) across three key areas:

1. Financial success—Is the company profitable?
2. Customer benefits—Does it genuinely add value to customers' lives?
3. Third-party impact—Does it contribute positively to society and the environment?

The results were then linked to each brand's Net Promoter Score (NPS)—a key metric that measures customer loyalty and likelihood to recommend a brand. The study

Perceived Purpose Scale

Financial success

> Profits for the company
> Financial security for the shareholders of the company
> Cost efficiency of the company

Customer benefits

> Solving customer problems
> User experience
> Safety for the customers and users

Third-party effects

> Ecologically and socially sustainable investment of the company's profits
> Solution to social and ecological problems
> Positive contribution to the community

found that brands perceived as caring about third-party impact often had stronger NPS scores, suggesting that doing good can also be good for business. It's an interesting way to quantify brand purpose and show that consumer perception plays a huge role in long-term success!

A clear purpose is crucial in a message because it helps connect with the audience on a deeper level, fostering trust, loyalty, and differentiation, ultimately driving brand success.

Here are some powerful aspects that make brand purpose so important:

- **Deeper Connection:** A clear purpose allows brands to communicate their values and beliefs, resonating with customers who share those same values.

- **Differentiation:** In a crowded marketplace, a unique purpose helps a brand stand out and establish its identity, making it memorable and recognizable.

- **Building Trust:** When a brand demonstrates a genuine commitment to its purpose, it builds trust and credibility with its audience, leading to stronger customer relationships.

- **Driving Loyalty:** Customers are more likely to become loyal to brands that align with their values and beliefs, making a purpose-driven brand more likely to retain customers.

- **Enhancing Customer Experience:** A strong brand purpose can enhance the customer experience by providing a sense of meaning and purpose behind the products or services offered.

- **Guiding Strategy:** A well-defined purpose serves as a compass, guiding brand strategy, communications, and marketing efforts, ensuring consistency and coherence.

- **Attracting Talent:** A compelling purpose can

also attract and retain employees who are passionate about the brand's mission.

In summary, brand purpose isn't just the "why" behind
a brand: it's the fuel for growth, the bedrock of authenticity, and the driving force for lasting social and economic
impact. Purpose-driven engagement is the Holy Grail of
Marketing, transforming simple transactional interactions
into trusted relationships that benefit the brand and its customers. In today's crowded market, purpose is the ultimate
differentiator, ensuring brands remain relevant, resilient,
and irreplaceable.

6

Right Environment

Delivering Your Message in the Optimal Environment

The channel your marketing message is being delivered in is an integral part of the message. The medium often becomes part of your message and can amplify your message exponentially (the medium or "messenger" has the potential to help, harm, or halt your message). Identifying and understanding your audience is critical to determining the medium of choice.

Despite media fragmentation that comes with consumers watching TV where and when they want, national television remains strong with the most expensive ads. The average cost for a thirty-second commercial during Super Bowl LIX in 2025 was $8 million. Is an ad this expensive, at a cost of $267,000 per second, worth it? Many pundits say yes. The Super Bowl is the most-viewed show on TV with 2024 setting a record with over 127 million viewers (according to Nielsen Media Research) not to mention all the earned (free) media exposures that come with the socialization of Super Bowl ads.

The Super Bowl is a great example of how the environment in which an ad appears can become part of the message, providing a halo effect that surrounds and elevates your brand.

How can brands reach their target audiences within high engagement environments at scale? Simulmedia, a leading AI-driven video advertising platform helps brands target prequalified audiences across linear TV and streaming. Their TV+ platform offers marketers deep insights into target audience viewing habits to help deliver more efficient ad campaigns across high-engagement content environments.

TV+ leverages AI and big data to pinpoint where and when strategic audiences will be watching, ensuring maximum reach with minimal waste. Its predictive analytics and cross-channel insights help advertisers navigate market fragmentation by identifying the most efficient, high-engagement environments to place ads across multiple networks.

The platform you choose for your ad can make a huge difference in its success. It affects how many people see it, how they engage with it, and how they perceive your message.

Let's break it down:

1. Audience Reach and Targeting
   - Different platforms reach different people: Social media is great for connecting with younger audiences, while print ads tend to work better for older demographics.
   - Targeting specific locations: Digital ads let you focus on certain areas, interests, or behaviors, making it easier to reach the right audience.
   - How often people see your ad matters: The more exposure your ad gets, the more it helps build brand awareness.
2. Engagement and Message Delivery
   - Different formats create different experiences: A video ad on YouTube or Instagram

can be super engaging, while a print ad is better for detailed information.

- Interactivity boosts engagement: Social media and websites allow for things like interactive ads, surveys, and call-to-action buttons, making it easier to engage with your audience.
- Trust matters: Some platforms have more credibility than others, which can shape how people perceive your ad and brand.

3. Cost and Budget
   - Pricing varies across platforms: Digital ads can be budget-friendly and highly targeted, while traditional options like TV and print can be pricier but offer a much broader reach.

At the end of the day, the best platform depends on your audience, your message, and your budget. Choose wisely, and your ad will have a much bigger impact!

CHIPOTLE'S USE OF TECHNOLOGY TO BUILD THEIR BRAND

Chipotle Mexican Grill ("Chipotle") is also an example of a brand utilizing technology to engage with its customers via their preferred medium, its app. This quick-service restaurant (QSR) has a loyal following and often "drops" free chips, guacamole, drinks, or queso offers into its app for their most loyal Chipotle rewards members. Chipotle's primary way of engaging with its community about these incentives is through its app. The user receives an app notification that a free promotional item awaits in the member's app "Rewards" section. Messaging for this type of promotion reads, "Hey, it's been a while! We just dropped a sweet promo in your rewards section of the app. Check it out."

Email is also used to notify the Chipotle community of these exclusive offers. Apps offer a controlled environment to strengthen engagement through rewards for a brand's most important customers.

Chipotle also utilizes TV spots to emphasize its fresh ingredients and foods prepared daily in-store but relies on its app for pushing consumer-specific promotions with limited redemption windows of a few days. Given the popularity of its menu and easy-to-navigate app, Chipotle is a brand that serves offers to its customers where they are most receptive (in app), incentivizes them with the free food item, and thus is likely to retain those customers as brand enthusiasts.

A Case Study With 1-800-Flowers

1-800 Flowers uses loyalty programs and brand collaborations within high-engagement environments across email, apps, and their website to ensure growth and gain increased loyalty and purchases from their customers.

Jim McCann, the founder and chairman of 1-800-Flowers.com, which includes well-known brands such as Harry & David®, PersonalizationMall.com®, Cheryl's Cookies®, The Popcorn Factory®, Things Remembered®, and Smart-Gift Inc., believes that innovation and adaptability are key to staying relevant in today's fast-paced world.

"At 1-800-Flowers, we've transformed from a collection of specialty brands into a unique e-commerce platform that inspires our customers to give more, connect more, and build meaningful relationships. Since starting this company, we've always been committed to innovation. We want to be there for our customers whenever and wherever they need us, and we stay ahead of the curve by understanding that technology drives consumer behavior. We keep a close eye on new innovations to better engage with our customers. AI plays a big part in personalizing the customer experience and helping people to connect and build better relationships. For instance, our automated reminders ensure customers never miss important milestones like

birthdays and anniversaries. We've also introduced fun AI tools like MomVerse and DadJoke GPT, which let customers create personalized songs, poems, verses, and jokes for Mother's Day and Father's Day. As we look to the future, we'll keep exploring new opportunities to leverage innovative technologies, always focusing on how they can bring more value to our customers and the environments we show up in. Our mission is to help our community of customers create better and more meaningful relationships. We're always looking for ways to help people express themselves with their loved ones. Giving is the gift, and we're creating a platform that inspires connection and meaningful relationships. We've been expanding our offerings in many exciting ways."

McCann continues, "We've introduced curated bundles

like Blossoms & Wine, Gourmet Drizzled Strawberries & Wine, and Cake Pops with Drizzled Berries. We also offer gifts at varying price points to make gifting accessible for everyone."

"Our relationship marketing capabilities are expanding through exciting collaborations with brands like LoveShackFancy, Lionsgate, Barbie, NFL, and NCAA. We're experimenting with new formats like live shopping events and leveraging emerging technologies such as AI. We see great potential in positioning ourselves as a 365-day gifting destination and continuing to educate consumers about our multibrand offerings. Long-term, we're focusing on growing our Gourmet Food & Gift Baskets and personalization businesses as everyday gifting options. On the floral side, we continue to lead the market and seek to grow our share. We're also excited about the potential in our cross-brand purchasing capabilities on our platform, which will continue to be a key driver of growth moving forward."

Jason John, chief marketing officer at 1-800 Flowers shares, "Our focus is to give our community the greatest gift of all—the chance to create better and more meaningful relationships. We're always looking for ways to help people express themselves with their loved ones. Giving is the gift, and we're creating a platform that inspires people to connect with others and build meaningful relationships. A key

CELEBRATIONS℠
PASSPORT

way we've built a loyal customer base is by providing a variety of support and resources consumers need to nurture their relationships. For example, we've created guides on how to write a sympathy card because we know these are moments when finding the right words can be tough. For Mother's Day, we introduced MomVerse, an AI-powered poem and song generator that customers could use for free, and for Father's Day, we launched DadJoke GPT, a fun tool that created dad jokes for free. Another way we're building loyalty is through our Celebrations Passport loyalty program. This program rewards customers and celebrates their thoughtfulness with free standard shipping and no service charge for one full year on purchases made across our portfolio of brands and provides the ability to unlock additional perks and benefits that grow as members gift."

"We also offer a variety of helpful blog content, like tips on how to care for your flowers, gifting etiquette based on the occasion, and more. Additionally, Jim McCann, writes

a letter to our community of customers every Sunday afternoon called 'Celebrations Pulse.' These letters aren't about selling anything; instead, they share ways for our customers to build better relationships. We regularly invite readers to share their own stories, and Jim often shares many of them in subsequent letters. Over the past three years, we've created a community flywheel within a high-engagement environment that keeps getting stronger."

John goes on to share that their content, blogs, and influencer campaigns have enabled them to achieve over 127 million nontransactional consumer engagements. "We know that customers who engage with our content convert 300 to 500 basis points higher than those who don't. Through product expansion, creative collaborations, engaging content, and more, we attracted more than five million new customers in the past year."

CONTEXT IS A DRIVING FORCE TO ACHIEVING
THE HOLY GRAIL OF MARKETING

One of the most powerful truths I've uncovered in the pursuit of marketing's Holy Grail is that context is a driving force to achieving the Holy Grail of Marketing.

MediaScience is a leader in media and advertising innovation research. Having started as the Disney Media and Advertising Lab, their team has been reshaping how we understand media effectiveness. Their research reinforces a belief I've held for years: the environment in which your message appears doesn't just *support* your communication— it *transforms* it.

Let's put this into perspective. According to Media-Science, ads placed in premium digital environments deliver 2.4 times better recall and 1.6 times higher brand lift than those scattered across run-of-the-internet sites. And for light buyers—those elusive consumers who hold the key to real brand growth—the difference is even more dramatic: 3 times the recall, and 2.8 times the brand lift. That's not incremental improvement—that's a seismic shift in effectiveness.

The moving image is a particularly fascinating example.

In high-quality, short-form video environments, ads see 1.8 times better recall than Facebook video, and 2.8 times better brand lift than standard internet placements. Why? Because attention is earned, not assumed—and premium environments command it.

Marketing is not just about the message, but about *engineering the moment.* When the right message meets the right mindset, magic happens.

Nowhere is that more evident than in news media and Broadcaster Video on Demand (BVOD). MediaScience found that combined news formats are twice as effective as Facebook formats when it comes to unaided recall. And with BVOD, not only do consumers remember the ads more—they actually *enjoy* them more compared to when the same ad runs on YouTube or Facebook. That's context at work. It doesn't just carry the message—it elevates it.

Phillip Lomax, EVP at MediaScience shares, "when you put a brand message in a premium context, high-trust environment, the impact isn't just better—it's exponential. Context enriches content. It creates a halo effect that makes the message stick, resonate, and drive action. Further, context impacts the perceptions of brands in terms of trust and excitation.

And it's not just about digital versus traditional—it's

about *orchestration.* Lomax shares further that, "in Me-diaScience's 'Digital Loves TV' case study with Comcast Advertising, brands that integrated both TV and digital campaigns saw a 12 percent increase in brand lift and a 15 percent boost in recall, along with greater visual atten-tion with viewers watching 2.7x longer than digital ads. Alignment across channels, working together to create out-comes that no single touchpoint could achieve alone. We use different platforms because they do different things for us, they are tools in the marketer's toolkit."

So, here's my challenge to you: stop thinking of media as just the delivery mechanism. Start thinking of it as part of the message. Because when you get the context right, the mes-sage doesn't just land—it lingers, influences, and converts.

KEY RECOMMENDATIONS FOR CHOOSING AN EFFECTIVE MARKETING ENVIRONMENT

Here are some key recommendations for ensuring your marketing message appears in an effective environment:

1. Align the Medium with Your Audience
   - Choose platforms where your target au-dience naturally engages (e.g., Gen Z on

TikTok, professionals on LinkedIn, DIY enthusiasts on Pinterest).

- Understand audience behavior and consumption habits: Do they prefer short-form videos, in-depth articles, or interactive content?

2. Leverage Contextually Relevant Environments
   - Ensure your message appears in settings that enhance its credibility (e.g., a sustainability campaign on National Geographic vs. a random banner ad).
   - Partner with media outlets, influencers, or brands that share your values and reinforce your message.

3. Choose Platforms that Amplify Your Message
   - Social media platforms with high engagement (e.g., Instagram for visuals, Twitter for conversations, YouTube for storytelling).
   - Native advertising and sponsored content that blends seamlessly with organic content.
   - High-authority sites or publications that enhance trust.

4. Avoid Platforms that Can Dilute or Undermine Your Message
   - Steer clear of controversial, spammy, or

irrelevant environments that could harm your brand's reputation.

- Use brand safety tools to prevent ads from appearing next to negative or inappropriate content.

5. Optimize for Different Mediums

- Adapt your message for each platform (e.g., concise tweets vs. long-form LinkedIn posts).
- Use visuals, video, and interactive content to maximize impact.
- A/B test different placements to see where your message resonates best.

6. Leverage Influencers and Trusted Messengers

- Work with authentic influencers who align with your brand values and speak to your audience.
- Consider industry experts or user-generated content to enhance credibility.

7. Ensure Message Consistency Across Channels

- Keep branding and core messaging consistent, but tailor content for different mediums.
- Use cross-channel integration (e.g., linking a social campaign to a landing page or in-store experience).

8. Monitor Performance and Adjust

- Track engagement, conversion rates, and sentiment analysis to see if your message is resonating.
- Continuously optimize your strategy based on data insights.

By strategically choosing the right environment to share your message, you can amplify its reach, strengthen brand perception, and drive meaningful engagement.

7

Right Time

Timing is Everything!

I learned about effective marketing techniques as a young boy growing up in a household of seven kids. I loved sneakers! My oldest brother used to say that I always had the best pair in the family. How did this happen? It was all timed! I had to win over my mother before my siblings came home from school. I often tore out pictures of the sneakers I liked from magazine ads and displayed them on the kitchen table. I knew that reaching my mom at the right time with the right message in the right environment when she was not distracted by our considerable family chaos would win me the new pair of stylish sneakers I loved!

TIMING IS EVERYTHING

I share this example because at the most basic level timing is simple, along with being a critical marketing component to being successful. Without good timing, in an instant all your amazing work and marketing efforts can become counterproductive.

You've heard the cliché, "Timing is everything." Capturing the consumer at the exact moment that their interests, needs, and desires are present is critical. Combining that speed with contextual relevance makes all the difference for optimal engagement.

AI, near-field communication (NFC), time-based data, and social media offer the ability to time a message to when a potential customer is likely to have optimal interest and a need for your product or service. Returning to my example in the introduction about *when* Wendy's messaged me about that delicious chicken sandwich—it was *before* lunchtime because they anticipated my hunger. They found me right before my time of need.

Another instance that brings contextual relevance to life is when I was researching trampolines to buy for my son's birthday. The day after my online search, I was using Evite to create a party invitation. It couldn't have been a couple of seconds before ads for trampolines were popping up on the Evite page. The brands I had been researching were now lighting up my screen with a fireworks show of ads. I hadn't purchased a trampoline yet, so this timely presentation filled with various incentives and offers helped me when I was ready to make my decision. And I made the right decision—my son and his friends continue to enjoy our backyard trampoline!

GOOD TIMING AND THE HOLY GRAIL OF MARKETING FRAMEWORK APPLIES TO ALL BUSINESSES

The Holy Grail of Marketing is powerful and applies to all types of businesses. I was having a glass of wine this past weekend with my neighbor, Jon, a top personal injury lawyer. I asked jon about how he successfully grew his practice.

Jon is of Portuguese descent and speaks four languages: English, Portuguese, Spanish, and Italian. He grew up in Elizabeth, New Jersey, the hometown that HBO's super successful series *The Sopranos* was based on. After graduating from Brooklyn Law School, Jon went to work for an independent, Italian, personal injury lawyer.

He was successful from the onset, bringing in many new clients from his family and friends network. His Swiss Army Knife asset was being multilingual and social. When an accident happens, people are stressed and are drawn to professionals they can speak easily to and feel comfortable with.

After Jon had worked for his mentor for two years he decided to go off on his own with his brother. At this time, the field of personal injury lawyers had grown significantly. While their practice started off strong, their business began to plateau. Jon remembers a friend asking him at the time if he would invest in targeted advertising. One new client a week could be as much as $200,000+ in legal rewards. He started with a local investment using Google AdWords and search engine optimization (SEO) with ads in Spanish. This did ok but he was not seeing the ROI he set out to achieve. Jon then learned about a method that would become, to this day, his most successful form of advertising.

In 2002, a new law, the Open Public Records Act (OPRA), went into effect. This law made police accident reports, permits, etc. publicly open to everyone. Some municipalities even provided crash docs from the police reports. This report provided weekly car accident statistics for the local area. Needless to say, these reports provided optimal timing for Jon to reach the right prospective clients when they might have a need for a personal injury lawyer.

Jon began using this data from OPRA to send out letters by priority mail with next day delivery to people who had recently been in a car accident. They went further to narrow the data down to people who were passengers in a car accident, were not at fault, and would most likely have a viable personal injury case.

These letters were regulated with guidelines that required them to include legal bylines that stated clearly that the letter was an advertisement, including full transparency that their data was received through the OPRA act. This disclaimer was not only mandatory in their letter but was also required to be on the outside of the envelope. Instantly, the ROI was there! They immediately saw a positive return on investment with these targeted letters.

Over the years, they made their letters oversized and in color which was more costly but proved to be more effective. Today, the cost of each letter is as much as $25, including postage.

People responded to the letters at all times of the day. Once, Jon went into the office on a Saturday and two passengers who had received their targeted letter/advertisement and were rear-ended the week before called into his office and became large payout clients. If Jon had not been in the office that day to answer their call, they likely would have called and gone with another law firm. Jon and his brother realized that people wanted to talk to a live person and hired a bilingual answering service that would pick up calls 24/7. They provided the answering service with a two-part script—one script for new clients and one for existing clients. What's your name? When did the accident happen? How did you hear about us? How did the accident happen? The answering service sent Jon and his brother a text and email with a screening report of the call. When they received the report, they called any potentially viable cases back right away before another attorney could respond. Instantly, the ROI was there.

Being in a hypercompetitive field, Jon had to be creative and harness the most effective methods and technologies for reaching his most sought after customers in the most timely and relevant ways. His efforts resulted in him reaching the right person with the right message at the right time. This iterative process continues to power Jon and his brother's growth and success.

Together, contextual relevance and immediacy is unprecedented in how it can dramatically accelerate a brand's success. Even more, the Holy Grail of Marketing can alter the playing field for brands in what seemed impossible ways a short time ago. What marketers took months and years, even decades, to accomplish with their campaigns and activities is now actionable in an instant. That trust and loyalty can also be erased in an instant with the click of a button if the Holy Grail of Marketing isn't implemented in the right way.

RIGHT TIMING IS IMPORTANT FROM THE SELLER'S POINT OF VIEW

Another critical aspect of your message is its *time validity*. When I originally looked at the Holy Grail of Marketing framework, my focus was mainly on reaching the consumer at the right time for the consumer. However, when dealing with a scarce commodity, a crucial factor to timing often bears down on the seller and provider of the product or service. This important aspect of message timing came up during my conversation with Global CMO at VistaJet Matteo Atti who was featured earlier in Chapter 4. "There

is absolutely no point reaching somebody and suggesting that they should charter a jet for a trip from Singapore to NYC if that aircraft is not available for their trip. Our jets are constantly en route, so we have to make sure our planes are available for any itineraries we promote and at the time of demand—be it a business trip or a flight to the US Open. Being timely with your message becomes very important because there's nothing worse than advertising your services to a high-caliber client to fly to an important business meeting or a special occasion, only to find out it's not available. Luckily, our Members have guaranteed aircraft availability—so this is never a problem for them!"

LOYALTY MARKETING PLAYS AN IMPORTANT PART IN ACHIEVING GOOD TIMING

The Holy Grail of Marketing framework continues after the consumer becomes a customer.

Loyalty marketing is an important area related to timing. Growing business from your customer base is often when the stakes are highest. A common focus for brands is often referred to as the 80/20 rule where 80 percent of sales are driven by 20 percent of their customers. Reaching your most important customers at the right time with the right messaging creating customer loyalty is a multibillion-dollar area of marketing also referred to as customer relationship marketing (CRM). Think of massively successful CRM companies such as Salesforce and Oracle. Larry Ellison who was one of the founders of Oracle purchased an island not too long ago and has a net worth of over $185 Billion.

HALLMARK'S AND AMERICAN EXPRESS'S USE OF TECHNOLOGY TO STRENGTHEN CUSTOMER LOYALTY

Hallmark, the iconic family-run greeting card company based in Kansas City, Missouri, has embraced technology to help enhance its marketing and drive sales. Its free Crown Rewards loyalty program offers seasonal and monthly coupons for cards, holiday merchandise, and home decor—available not only in Hallmark stores but also through national partners like The Paper Store.

For years, Hallmark mailed both paper and email coupons to its loyalty members, often causing confusion due to timing discrepancies. In 2024, it streamlined the experience with its new Cards Now app, featuring a clean interface that centralizes digital coupons, rewards, and a unique barcode for easy in-store use. The app's home screen welcomes users with: *"Send paper cards by mail, or an e-card by text or email!"*

Additionally, Hallmark now sends exclusive text message promotions to opt-in Crown Rewards members. These single-channel offers—delivered only via text rather than the app or email—serve as direct purchase incentives. To further encourage repeat shopping, members receive a free monthly "Just Because" card, increasing in-store visits and engagement.

By leveraging app-based rewards, text promotions, and strategic incentives, Hallmark demonstrates its deep understanding of customer habits and technology use. Each text promotion is clear and action-driven, featuring direct links like "SHOP NOW" or "GET STARTED" to seamlessly guide consumers from promotion to purchase.

Another great example of well-timed messaging is the American Express app. Cardholders can browse and add exclusive promotions to their rewards account for future use. When location services are enabled, the app sends real-time notifications if the user is near a participating merchant, making it easy to take advantage of available offers. Additionally, push notifications serve as timely reminders to use saved promotions at nearby vendors, including restaurants, fast food chains, and retail stores—ensuring cardholders never miss a deal.

THE GROWTH OF LOYALTY MARKETING

In June 2024, the Association of National Advertisers (ANA) which is the US advertising industry's oldest, most reputable, and largest trade association launched a survey to understand loyalty marketing in order to learn more about its benefits, challenges, and any concerns about fraud.

Loyalty marketing rewards customers for their repeat purchases or interactions with a brand. The ANA study found that loyalty marketing is increasingly an important part of a brand's marketing campaigns. The majority of their survey respondents expect loyalty marketing to be more important in the next year for their organization, compared with the recent past. According to the study's qualitative discussions, loyalty marketing provides brands the ability to collect customer data and insights and market directly to customers—and often loyalty members are a brand's best customers. The study also found that consumers are increasingly signing up for loyalty programs to find value and fight inflation.

ANA's CMO Growth Council has identified four global growth priorities and a twelve-point industry growth agenda. Loyalty marketing fits under the Brand, Creativity, and Media growth priority within the Brand/Marketing Innovation area of focus. Loyalty marketing also fits under

the Data, Technology, and Measurement growth priority under the Data, Analytics, and Technology area of focus as seen in the image below.

AI AND NFC ARE OPTIMIZING MARKETING

Below is a summary of key benefits to combining AI and NFC:

Real-Time Data Processing

- Immediate Insights: AI processes data in real time, enabling marketers to react instantly to consumer actions and trends.
- Dynamic Adjustments: Campaigns can be adjusted on the fly based on real-time performance metrics and feedback.

Synergy of AI and NFC in Marketing

1. Hyper-personalization
   - AI-Driven Insights: AI analyzes NFC data to understand consumer behavior in specific locations and contexts, enabling hyperpersonalized marketing messages.
   - Tailored Experiences: Combined, AI and NFC can deliver highly relevant content and offers precisely when and where the consumer is most receptive.
2. Real-Time Engagement
   - Immediate Reactions: AI processes NFC-triggered interactions in real time, allowing marketers to engage with consumers instantly with personalized messages.

- Contextual Relevance: The combination ensures that marketing efforts are contextually relevant, increasing effectiveness and customer satisfaction.

3. Optimized Campaigns
   - Data Integration: AI integrates data from NFC interactions with other data sources to provide a comprehensive view of consumer behavior.
   - Continuous Improvement: Marketers can continuously optimize campaigns based on detailed insights from both AI and NFC data.

By integrating AI and NFC technologies, marketers can create highly targeted, timely, and relevant marketing strategies that enhance customer engagement and drive better results.

KEY RECOMMENDATIONS FOR KEEPING YOUR MARKETING CONTEXTUALLY RELEVANT AND REACHING THE RIGHT AUDIENCE

Here are some key tips for ensuring your ads and marketing efforts are contextually relevant and resonate with the right audience at the right time:

1. Leverage Data & Insights
   - Use real-time data to understand consumer behavior, preferences, and purchase intent.
   - Analyze browsing history, location, and search trends to deliver more personalized content.
2. Use Geotargeting & Location-Based Marketing
   - Tailor ads based on a user's location to provide relevant offers (e.g., Burger King's "Whopper Detour" campaign).
   - Utilize geo-fencing to engage customers near competitors or specific stores.
3. Align with Consumer Intent
   - Ensure messaging matches the user's stage in the buying journey.
   - Provide helpful content when consumers are actively researching products or services.
4. Tap into the Right Platforms at the Right Time
   - Serve ads on platforms where users are most engaged (e.g., social media, search engines, and email).
   - Use contextual placements, such as displaying relevant ads while users browse related content (e.g., trampoline ads appearing on an Evite page for a birthday party).

5. Personalize Your Messaging
   - Use AI and machine learning to tailor content, recommendations, and offers based on past interactions.
   - Address consumers by name and reference their preferences, when possible.

6. Use Dynamic & Adaptive Content
   - Create dynamic ads that adjust in real time based on user data and behavior.
   - Test different creatives and headlines to see what resonates best with different segments.

7. Consider the Customer's Emotions & Environment
   - Be mindful of timing—avoid intrusive or poorly timed ads that could feel out of place.
   - Align messaging with current events, seasons, and consumer mindsets.

8. Optimize for Mobile & Omnichannel Experiences
   - Ensure ads and content are mobile-friendly and seamlessly integrated across platforms.
   - Use push notifications, SMS marketing, and email retargeting to stay top-of-mind.

9. Incorporate AI & Automation

- Use AI-driven recommendations and auto-mated bidding strategies to reach users when they are most likely to engage.
- Implement chatbots and interactive content to create personalized experiences.

10. Measure & Adjust for Continuous Improvement
    - Track key metrics (CTR, conversion rates, engagement) to assess performance.
    - A/B test different ad formats, messaging, and placements to optimize relevance and effectiveness.

8

Bad Outcomes

What Can Happen When the Holy Grail of
Marketing is Not Being Used Effectively

I t's more challenging than ever to be an effective marketer. Consumers are in the driver's seat with unprecedented control, choosing when and where to engage with media across multiple screens and formats. Marketers must take a holistic, integrated approach to meet these challenges and ensure messaging continuity and safety across platforms.

Achieving the Holy Grail of Marketing requires delivering on every framework component—each part is crucial. For example, you may have utilized deep audience insights to create a highly effective campaign. However, if your ad runs in environments that are misaligned with your brand image or have low engagement, all the great work of reaching the right person with the right message at the right time goes out the window.

Let's look at a few cases where marketing campaigns have fallen short because they failed to deliver the right message in the right contextual environment.

NIKE'S "WINNING ISN'T FOR EVERYONE" CAMPAIGN

Nike's "Winning Isn't for Everyone" 2024 Summer Olympics campaign, inspired by its athletes, emphasized a relentless drive to win. The campaign speaks to the determination and sacrifice that Olympic athletes claim are required in order to win and that sets them apart from their competition. However, this messaging came off as overly harsh and alienating. The ad's voiceover included lines like, "I have no empathy. I don't respect you. I'm never satisfied." Billboards in cities worldwide paired athletes with copy such as, "If you don't want to win, you've already lost" and "My dream is to end theirs." These statements painted a picture of winning at all costs, without empathy or respect for others.

While the ads reached the right audience—sports enthusiasts watching the Olympics—the messaging was out of sync with the values of this unifying global event, such as excellence, compassion, and innovation. Rather than inspiring viewers, the tone promoted a win-at-all-costs mentality that felt off-putting.

With such a strong track record of positive, motivational advertising, Nike's Olympic message felt off-brand and lacked resonance and approval on a wide scale. (Author note: Gaining sales from the campaign would also be challenging; except for a few new shoe editions, many of Nike's latest innovations won't hit stores until 2025, limiting the campaign's immediate Olympic-oriented impact).

Nike's campaign illustrates that the wrong message can undermine a brand's efforts even when reaching the right audience in the right environment. The idea of winning resonated with Olympic viewers, but it should have been delivered in a way that aligned with the event's spirit. We know Nike can do it as seen in Chapter 4 with the success of their gender-equality Super Bowl ad.

PEPSI'S "LIVE FOR NOW" CAMPAIGN

When Pepsi launched a commercial featuring supermodel Kendall Jenner posing against the backdrop of a peaceful demonstration to support the Black Lives Matter movement, the ad was meant to resonate with millennials with a message of relevance and unity but was met immediately with condemnation. Critics accused Pepsi and Jenner of making light of the Black Lives Matter movement and police brutality. The backlash was so swift that Pepsi pulled the ad within forty-eight hours.

The ad features Jenner watching what appears to be a protest taking place outside her photo shoot. Young people are marching, carrying signs that say "peace" and "love" in what seems to be a party-like atmosphere. Jenner heads toward the demonstration and walks to the front, where several white police officers are standing in a line, offering a can of Pepsi to one of the officers as a symbolic peace offering.

The commercial sparked outrage for its tone-deaf and insensitive portrayal of protests. The carefree, celebratory scene felt out of touch with the gravity of real-life demonstrations, where people potentially lose their lives fighting for social justice.

Bernice King, the daughter of Martin Luther King Jr., tweeted in response, "If only Daddy would have known about the power of #Pepsi." This sentiment echoed across social media, underscoring the public's frustration with the ad's misjudgment.

Pepsi apologized, stating the ad was intended to project "a global message of unity, peace, and understanding" and acknowledging they had "missed the mark." The lesson here is clear: entering polarized or sensitive social conversations without a deep understanding of the context can ruin a brand's reputation. Brands need to be careful about engaging in controversy. An immediate backlash from a disgruntled audience can translate into losing customers' trust and business.

IMPORTANCE OF CRAFTING THE RIGHT MESSAGE

The Pepsi and Nike examples demonstrate the importance of getting the message right. Incorporating diverse perspectives during the creative process and thoroughly assessing potential risks is essential and can't be overstated. Marketers must also go beyond brainstorming and strategy sessions, employing available data, insights, and tools like social listening to gauge public sentiment. This can help make or break the message, avoiding tone-deaf imagery and copy and ensuring campaigns resonate with the intended audience.

THE ROLE OF AD VIEWABILITY & PLACEMENT

The placement of advertising can have various pitfalls. Marketers can have crafted the right audience message and chosen the right time but the viewability and placement are misaligned. This process can happen for multiple reasons and cause immense harm to the brand.

Let's start with ad fraud. Bots (software that acts like human impressions) or fraudulent websites can generate fake impressions, clicks, or engagement, and the practice is only expected to accelerate with the adoption and advancement of AI and other emerging, data-driven technology. This ad deception misleads marketers into thinking their ads are performing well when, in fact, they're not reaching real people.

VIEWABILITY AND AD FRAUD ARE KEY METRICS RELATED TO THE QUALITY OF PROGRAMMATIC BUYS

- Viewability shows whether a consumer had the opportunity to see an ad. According to industry standards, a display ad will be counted as

viewable if at least 50 percent of its area is vis-
ible for a minimum of one second on the user's screen and a minimum of two seconds for a
video ad.

- Digital advertising fraud (more specifically
  known as invalid traffic or IVT) has been a
  persistent challenge for the industry. While advertisers expect their content will be viewed by
  legitimate consumers with the potential to buy
  their products and services, criminal organizations have attacked the digital ad ecosystem and
  defrauded legitimate participants in the supply
  chain. As a result, advertisers may end up pay-
  ing a material portion of their campaign dollars
  to criminals who generate ad impressions that
  are never seen by legitimate consumers.

THE RISKS TO AUTOMATED ADVERTISING

Even the best campaigns can succeed only if placed in appropriate environments. Today, ad campaigns are increasingly automated by programmatic advertising platforms.
Automation can lower costs and increase efficiency but can
also be detrimental when ads appear across unwarranted

environments. Programmatic platforms use algorithms to target users. These algorithms analyze vast amounts of user data to determine what ads to show, increasing the chance of viewer engagement. While these algorithms can be effective, they can also fail to account for the context and placement in which the ad is shown. This can result in a "spray and pray" approach that can negatively affect your campaign's outcome.

As more advertising gets digitized, fraud will worsen within the digital ecosystem. Between 2018 and 2025, digital ad fraud is projected to grow from $35 billion to over $100 billion, per Statista.

The Association of National Advertisers' (ANA) 2023 Programmatic Media Supply Chain Transparency Study estimated that in the $88 billion open web programmatic ecosystem some $22 billion is wasteful or unproductive. That amounts to *one in four dollars*—a massive opportunity loss. ANA cited this as being driven by a lack of data access and transparency, prioritizing cost over value, and other inefficiencies throughout the process.

The ANA also noted that Made for Advertising (MFA) websites in the study represented 21 percent of impressions and 15 percent of spend. MFA sites typically use sensational headlines, clickbait, and provocative content to attract visitors and generate page views, which in turn generate ad revenue for the site owner. MFA sites also usually feature low-quality content and may use tactics such as pop-up ads, auto-play videos, or intrusive ads to maximize ad revenue.

The ANA included in their study multiple steps to overcoming programmatic ad buying inefficiencies and waste, including:

- Know, and then optimize, the number of websites being used for your programmatic campaigns. If the number of websites is high (and the average of 44,000 among ANA study participants is indeed high), consider a focus on trusted sellers (partners known for their credibility and reliability in the programmatic ecosystem). Optimizing the number of websites will diminish the risk of purchasing non-viewable and fraudulent inventory and enhance brand safety.
- Advertisers should recognize that MFA sites can account for a significant portion of their open web programmatic budget. Audit your activity to understand the percent of impressions and

spend represented by MFA sites. Advertisers should determine, independently, if MFA sites fit with their brand suitability standards for content and user experience and clarify their tolerance for the inclusion of MFA inventory in their campaigns.

- Buy through direct inventory supply paths. Directness matters. Most supply chains fork, and the primary seller may buy from a secondary seller. This not only adds cost but also starts breaking filtrations that are in place for viewability, IVT, brand safety, and inclusion. Importantly, each additional hop to a new supplier drives up your carbon footprint.

- Advertisers are responsible for more active stewardship of their media investments. Media is often the largest marketing expenditure at most companies. Advertisers need to "lean in" and be more active stewards of their media investments rather than delegating that entirely to their outside agencies. Advertisers should appoint a chief media officer (either in title or function) who should take responsibility for the internal media management and governance processes that deliver performance, media accountability, and transparency throughout the programmatic media supply chain. Advertisers who outsource their media management without active internal stewardship do so at their own risk.

- Demand to understand the sustainability impact of programmatic media purchases. More productive buys can often lead to lower carbon emissions. The longer the supply chain, the higher the carbon emissions. Buy through direct inventory supply paths. Work with trusted sellers, and not resellers. Work with SSP partners that have direct connections to the publishers on your trusted seller list. Evaluate the role of MFA sites, which generate 26 percent more carbon emissions than non-MFA inventory. Concentrate programmatic media activity on a smaller number of curated websites.

AI MAY ALSO AID IN CREATING DEEPFAKES

AI may also aid in creating deepfakes (computer-generated images) and other forms of synthetic content, further complicating the identification of real versus fake user interactions. Marketers must implement more advanced fraud detection systems to combat this growing problem.

Marketing and ad fraud distort campaign metrics and drain budgets. The ANA study supports the lesson for marketers that they should be careful about the providers they do business with. They should become educated about the issues around ad fraud, conduct meticulous research, secure trusted referrals, and ask questions before enlisting a partner.

Ad placements can also be ineffective and sometimes detrimental through poor editorial placement targeting. Marketers can create the right message and identify the right audience. Still, the Holy Grail of Marketing only works if the ad is placed in a setting aligned with the brand's ethos, message, and image. Poorly targeted ads produce the wrong outcome. For instance, when an advertisement for a luxury product appears on a low-quality or irrelevant site, the brand's image is diluted.

Content mismatch also diminishes the likelihood of conversion due to the wrong impression and low engagement delivered. Proper targeting, authentic engagement, and transparency are vital to providing a positive ROI against a brand's advertising investment.

SOCIAL PLATFORMS DELIVERING BAD OUTCOMES REQUIRING HUMAN OVERSIGHT

Without human oversight, data-driven algorithms can bear detrimental effects. For example, TikTok and Meta, which owns Instagram, Facebook, Threads, and WhatsApp, have come under fire for exposing teens to weight loss supplements, fasting apps, unhealthy diet trends, cosmetic surgery, and glorifying unrealistic body standards that promote negative body image and contribute to mental health issues. In these instances, the consequences of reaching a young, impressionable audience have been extremely harmful on a large scale.

The behemoth platforms Meta, Snap, TikTok, and X have been scrutinized for promoting harmful advertising posts and calls for action and reform to reduce screen time and social media access among young people are intensifying as their use and volume are correlated with the rise in anxiety, depression, and suicidal ideation.

In addition to staying on top of these societal issues, marketers must balance ad placement and precision targeting practices with awareness and sensitivity to the audience's well-being. It's crucial to fully understand the gravity and depth that ad misalignment can present to their brand's image, their brand's reputation, and society as a whole. The serious nature of these issues is an opportunity for brands to step up and be positive forces of change.

FINAL THOUGHTS

Carefully focusing on the outcome that you want to achieve is necessary at the onset of an ad campaign in order to succeed. Achieving the Holy Grail of Marketing requires more than reaching the right person with the right message at the right time—it demands careful consideration of the environment in which the message is delivered as well as the technology and the automated programmatic platforms being used, with a keen respect for the audiences being targeted. All aspects of the Holy Grail of Marketing's framework must work together to be successful. One misstep can cause the entire campaign to fail. Successful marketing truly is equal to the sum of all its parts.

The Holy Grail of Marketing Translates into Optimal Sales

The Increased Convergence of Marketing and Sales

A top sales performer's number one attribute is the ability to not waste time and effort on the wrong clients who will never buy from them. The quote by Benjamin Franklin, "remember that time is money" applies to every sales role. It has never been more challenging to be a salesperson. Executives who are deciding what products and services to purchase are more strapped for time than ever and have high-performing spam filters to block unwanted sales pitches. At the same, it has never been a better time to be working in sales. With the help of advanced technologies, marketing teams are collaborating more closely with their sales teams to help them communicate with the right customers with the right message in the right environment at the right time s to deliver the right outcome—increased sales. Marketing teams are developing highly personalized marketing strategies, leveraging data analytics to identify ideal customer segments, and delivering targeted messages across various channels based on individual customer behaviors and needs, ensuring the communication is relevant to their current situation and pain points, ultimately increasing the likelihood of engagement and conversion.

TIME IS MONEY

No matter what you are selling—from a $50 per month cybersecurity software to a $30 million private jet—your ability to optimize your sales efforts by reaching the right person with the right message in the right environment at the right time will make or break your hitting your sales goal and your company succeeding.

As performance-driven digital marketing increasingly becomes a core discipline, marketers have expanded from being focused on creative branding to also being strategic drivers of business growth. By leveraging digital technologies and tactics like social media, SEO, and content marketing, brands can engage audiences with precision, enhance brand awareness, and foster meaningful customer interactions that drive increased sales.

COLLABORATION BETWEEN SALES AND MARKETING TEAMS IS A STRATEGIC NECESSITY

Collaboration between sales and marketing has evolved from a siloed approach to a strategic necessity driven by changes in customer behavior and technology. Sara Melefsky, an experienced digital marketing professional within the manufacturing industry, explains that "sales and marketing teams need to align on audience targeting, lead qualification, and content strategies to deliver a seamless customer experience. Tools like CRM systems and marketing automation enhance this synergy by streamlining lead management, personalizing messaging, and optimizing campaign performance, ultimately driving revenue and fostering long-term loyalty."

The transition to collaborative sales and marketing

efforts has improved lead quality by focusing on high-value prospects through data-driven segmentation and personalized communication. Marketing attracts and educates prospects with targeted content, while sales builds relationships, addresses pain points, and provides tailored solutions, sharing insights to refine strategies. This synergy enhances customer experiences across all touchpoints, boosting satisfaction, retention, and brand advocacy in a competitive market.

RISING CUSTOMER EXPECTATIONS IS ACCELERATING SALES AND MARKETING INTEGRATION

The integration of sales and marketing is accelerating to meet rising customer expectations. Melefsky shares that "agile practices and cross-functional collaboration enable teams to adapt swiftly to seize opportunities. By combining data-driven insights with human-centered strategies, organizations can build stronger customer relationships resulting in higher conversions and long-term drive growth."

During my consultancy for a leading UX (user experience) platform, one of my beauty e-commerce clients transitioned its website to dynamic interface pages which resulted in a 25 percent increase in conversions in the first six months. You might be asking yourself, what is a dynamic interface page? A dynamic interface site tracks individual's past purchasing and engagement data so that when the consumer returns to their website, the items that they previously purchased or hovered over appear on the home page. So, imagine you visited this beauty site last week and purchased rose-colored lipstick. The next time you visit the site, that rose-colored lipstick, now shown with matching nail polish, appears on the site's home page with a "click to purchase" button embedded in the content. This new customized, dynamic user experience increased conversions on their website like never before!

How does this apply to the Holy Grail of Marketing? The beauty site reached the right person through tracking historical engagement and purchasing data. The right message was delivered in real time on their site to match the consumers' interests and tastes. The right environment was their website where they had full control over the user experience. The right time was achieved by engaging the consumer when they revisited their website. And the right outcome was delivered with a drastic increase in conversions.

Let's also look at how sales and marketing teams can benefit from collaborating to apply the Holy Grail of Marketing framework.

SEAMLESS CUSTOMER EXPERIENCE
RESULTS IN LOYAL CUSTOMERS

When both sales and marketing teams align on buyer understanding, businesses can deliver a seamless customer experience, turning potential leads into loyal customers.

Melefsky shares how she was once told, "You will never be a good marketer if you never take the time to deeply understand every aspect of your buyer." In today's fast-changing world, where customers' needs and technology are constantly evolving, it's even more critical. "This means not just analyzing data to drive decisions but also stepping into the buying environment to truly understand how customers interact with the product and brand."

COLLABORATION IS ESSENTIAL
FOR STAYING AHEAD

By using tools like data analysis, automation, and CRM systems alongside firsthand insights gathered through direct customer engagement, teams can refine their strategies to ensure they reach the right people, with the right message, in the right environment, at the right time. "In today's competitive market, this kind of collaboration isn't just important—it's essential for driving sustainable growth and staying ahead," explains Melefsky.

It's imperative that marketers have a deep understanding of buyer behavior—not just from quantitative data and insights, but through a genuine, qualitative understanding of who the buyers are and how they interact with the product and brand. Often, sales teams have a stronger grasp of this behavior because they are in the field, engaging directly with customers on a daily basis. They observe firsthand how buyers make decisions, navigate a shopping experience, and interact with products. This frontline perspective is key to implementing the Holy Grail of Marketing method.

Melefsky shares the analogy of being a marketing manager for a cosmetics company: "It's easy to rely on data pulled from past campaigns and research programs to say, I know how our buyers behave in the store and what they want. But when was the last time you stood in the aisles and watched potential buyers engage with your products? Observing how they move through the store, which products they pick up, and what they focus on can reveal far more than a set of numbers."

Taking a step into your customers' world is essential for crafting impactful marketing campaigns. Melefsky recommends that sales and marketing teams should both act as "secret shoppers," getting involved in the buying environment. Observe how buyers engage with your products: where their eyes land on the shelves, what catches their attention, how they handle the products, and even what they do when they put a product back on the shelf. When the moment feels right, engage them. Ask questions like, "What made you pick up that lipstick?"; "What were you hoping to see on the label?"; "Why did you decide to put it back and choose something else?"

UNDERSTANDING BUYER MOTIVATION IN REAL TIME RESULTS IN MEANINGFULLY TIMED MESSAGES

These insights provide critical information that can be supported by insights from data analytics. "Understanding the motivations and actions of buyers in real time offers a chance to refine your marketing efforts—whether it's improving the product itself, changing its placement, or even tweaking the messaging on the label or marketing materials. This hands-on research bridges the gap between the data and the experience of the buyer, allowing both marketing and sales to truly understand their audience. By stepping into the shoes of your customer, you gain the opportunity to create a more personalized, effective marketing strategy," explains Melefsky.

Great results are driven by marketing and sales teams collaborating and utilizing the Holy Grail of Marketing framework to develop campaigns that not only reach the right buyer but also resonate with them in meaningful ways at optimal purchasing moments, increasing the chances of converting them into loyal customers with the right outcome delivered!

10

Right Outcomes

Closing Thoughts

S o here we are at the final chapter. I hope that this book has opened your eyes to new ideas on how you can optimize your marketing campaigns and be more success-ful. One could argue that this chapter should have been the first chapter. As one of Stephen Covey's *Seven Habits of Highly Successful People* states, "Always begin with the end in mind."

My goal for this book is to make it the must-read modern-day marketing book by providing a guiding framework along with cutting-edge marketing applications to help you be successful within the complex and fast-paced marketing field.

This book was written for anyone accountable to a marketing budget—big or small. Anyone touching marketing has an entrepreneurial spirit. We all have passion for making something great. There's a saying that nothing happens until something is sold. I prefer the statement that "nothing is sold until an effective marketing framework is developed and acted upon with positive results."

When I originally came up with the framework for this book it included the following four components: Reaching the *Right Person* with the *Right Message* in the *Right Environment* at the *Right Time*. When I shared this framework with my teaching mentor, Sertan Kabadayi, who hired me ten years ago as an adjunct marketing professor at Fordham, he asked me if I thought about adding to the framework the *Right Outcome*. Professor Kabadayi went on to say that "there are brands that might be good at achieving the core framework but if the right outcome is not achieved it could actually create more detriment than good for a brand and our society at large." I knew immediately the importance of adding to the framework the "Right Outcome." The framework needs a bullseye to aim at. You can have the best bow and arrows but if the arrows miss the bullseye, you will quickly fail.

SUCCESS COMES WITH A KEEN UNDERSTANDING OF THE OUTCOME YOU WISH TO ACHIEVE

Success cannot be achieved without a keen understanding of the outcome you wish to receive, one which needs to be delivered with measurable results. Professor Kabadayi shared further that "limiting the impact of a marketing campaign solely for financial outcomes would be an unfair assessment of its true potential. Beyond driving business success, marketing has the power to enhance the well-being of individuals, communities, society, and the planet. More than just a tool for achieving financial goals, it can be leveraged to address the pressing challenges humanity faces. I firmly believe that creating meaningful outcomes for all should be an indispensable part of marketing's ultimate purpose and of Holy Grail Marketing—one that every marketer should strive to achieve."

Right Outcome: What do you want to achieve with your campaign? What is the result you are looking to achieve? What is the by-product? What do you want the audience to take away from engaging with your message?

ACHIEVING THE HIGHEST LEVEL OF MARKETING PERFORMANCE

The Holy Grail of Marketing is the highest level of marketing performance that is impossible to fully achieve. This is a guiding framework that acts as a foundation to enable you to strive for the highest performance possible. Marketing is an iterative process that is constantly evolving and adjusting to consumer shifts in behavior along with the many new marketing technologies that are constantly emerging.

As mentioned in Chapter 5 on the importance of brand purpose—a well-defined brand purpose isn't just a catchy slogan or marketing gimmick, it's the intrinsic foundation of a brand's identity, a strategic asset that fuels growth, drives positive social impact, and builds rock-solid loyalty.

Purpose captures a brand's unique value and how it enriches customers' lives. Without a clear purpose, brands risk becoming just another commodity, stuck in transactional relationships lacking the emotional connection that leads to brand champions and customers' long-term loyalty.

COURAGE MAKES MARKETERS SUCCESSFUL

Being a successful marketer takes courage. We all, at some point, will sit at the poker table asking for a stack of chips to make our bets on a marketing campaign we believe in and are passionate about. The Holy Grail of Marketing is your North Star to help minimize your risk while guiding you to new heights of success!

We are all accountable to someone—be it ourselves, our partner(s), our boss, and/or board of directors and shareholders. When I told my wife a few years ago that I wanted to launch my own innovative dog products website she said it "sounds like a nice idea but you're not investing our life savings in a website that is unproven and will never be able to compete against Amazon." I eventually convinced her to allow me to draw $5k from our life savings. Our agreement was clear, once the $5k was gone, that was it and the site was shutting down if not profitable. Boy did I need the Holy Grail of Marketing framework! I was now accountable and had to optimize every dollar I invested in marketing.

HOLISTIC APPROACH TO MARKETING

The Holy Grail of Marketing framework is a holistic approach for you to draw from no matter how complex and challenging things get. The cover of this book mentions AI and Beyond. Chapter 2 on how AI and data optimize the Holy Grail of Marketing framework provides you with insights on how to be effective with using new AI and data applications within your marketing plans. The "beyond" aspect is about how the Holy Grail of Marketing can contribute to your company's brand purpose and ethos that extend far beyond profits to contribute to societal good and endure across the lifetime of your brand.

With the rapid pace of AI advancements, we mustn't be intimidated or fearful but rather embrace the riches that AI and new technologies offer to our marketing campaigns. As Vera Hsu from Microsoft shared in Chapter 2, we have a great opportunity to upskill our employees and humanize our AI initiatives.

The Holy Grail of Marketing offers our brands a brighter future that delivers optimal results for both our bottom lines and a sustained future to contribute to a greater cause and make our world a better place.

May the many examples and case studies I shared in

this book provide you with the courage and creative ambition to take your brand to new heights never before imagined.

I wish you the very best with your marketing and life endeavors. Keep up-to-date with the Holy Grail of Marketing at www.holygrailofmarketing.com and on Linkedin at linkedin.com/in/greglicciardi.

Holy Grail of Marketing: Checklist & Key Recommendations

Chapter 1: Defining the Holy Grail of Marketing

✓ The Ultimate Goal – Deliver the right message, to the right person, in the right environment, at the right time to drive engagement, sales, and brand loyalty.

✓ Breaking Down Barriers – Brands that master this cut through noise, connect authentically, and create lasting customer relationships.

Chapter 2: AI & Data – Unlocking the Holy Grail of Marketing

✓ AI-Powered Insights – Use AI for hyper-personalization, predictive analytics, and automated content generation.

✓ Big Data for Targeting – Leverage customer data, browsing behavior, and purchase history to refine messaging.

✓ Automation & Machine Learning – Optimize ad placements, email timing, and recommendations for maximum impact.

Chapter 3: Reaching the Right Person

✓ Hyper-Targeting & Psychographics – Go beyond demographics; focus on lifestyles, values, and interests.

✓ Lookalike Audiences – Use existing customer data to find new, high-potential consumers.

✓ Segmentation for Maximum ROI – Customize messaging for niche audiences and high-intent buyers.

Chapter 4: Right Message –
The Message is King

✓ Clear, Customer-Centric Value – Speak to customer needs, emotions, and pain points.

✓ Brand Storytelling – Build trust and loyalty with authentic narratives.

✓ Call to Action (CTA) – Ensure messaging drives action (Buy Now, Sign Up, Learn More).

Chapter 5: Brand Purpose –
The Ultimate Differentiator

✓ Consumers Value Purpose – Brands with a clear mission stand out in crowded markets.

✓ Authenticity Matters – Align messaging with real actions (CSR initiatives, sustainability efforts, social impact).

✓ Purpose-Driven Brands Win – Companies that care about more than just profits build stronger customer connections.

Chapter 6: Right Environment –
Where Message Meets Impact

✓ Medium Enhances the Message – Choose platforms that amplify your brand's story (e.g., luxury brands on premium media).

✓ Omnichannel Marketing – Ensure a seamless experience across digital, social, and in-store touchpoints.

✓ Influencer & Partner Alignment – Work with voices that resonate with your audience.

Chapter 7: Right Time – Timing is Everything

✓ Behavior-Driven Triggers – Use AI to send messages when customers are most likely to engage.

✓ Location-Based Marketing – Deliver offers when customers are near your store or ready to buy.

✓ Seasonal & Event-Based Promotions – Align with key holidays, trends, and customer life moments.

Chapter 8: Bad Outcomes When the Holy Grail is Ignored

✗ Mismatched Audience & Message – Leads to low engagement, wasted ad spend, and missed opportunities.

✗ Poor Timing & Execution – Sending the right message at the wrong time fails to convert.

✗ Inauthentic Branding – Customers see through false brand purpose and disengage.

✗ Rely on programmatic automated ad campaigns - be cautious of ad fraud including wasted impressions on non-humans and ads appearing in harmful environments

Chapter 9: Achieving Optimal Sales & Success

✓ Personalization at Scale – Tailor experiences to individual customer preferences.

✓ Data-Driven Decisions – Use insights to refine messaging, optimize channels, and increase conversions.

✓ Customer-Centric Marketing – Focus on long-term relationships, not just transactions.

Chapter 10: Achieving the Right Outcome

✓ Begin with the End in Mind – Define your ultimate marketing goals before execution.

✓ Set Clear KPIs – Identify key performance indicators (KPIs) to measure success (e.g., conversions, engagement, ROI).

✓ Test, Learn & Optimize – Continuously analyze data, A/B test strategies, and adapt for better results.

✓ Long-Term Vision – Think beyond short-term wins and focus on sustainable brand growth and customer loyalty.

References

Introduction

Census.gov.

Chapter 1

"Harry's Shows It's Not the Biggest Marketing Budgets That Win." (2025). *Canva.*

https://www.canva.com/learn/harrys-shows-its-not-the -biggest-marketing-budgets-that-win.

Harrys.com.

Chapter 2

Weathercompany.com.

Chapter 4

Maslow's Hierarchy of Needs. *Wikipedia.* https://en.wiki
pedia.org/wiki/Maslow%27s_hierarchy_of_needs.

"2023 Sports Fan Insights: The Beginning of the Immersive
Sports Era."

Deloitte Center for Technology, Media & Telecom. (2023).
https://www2.deloitte.com/us/en/insights/industry/media
-and-entertainment/immersive-sports-fandom.html.

Amanda Christovich. (2022). "WNBA, Teams Valued at
$1B Following Capital Raise." *Front Office Sports.* https://
frontofficesports.com/wnba-teams-valued-at-1b-following
-capital-raise/.

SponsorUnited. (2022). Women in Sports Sponsorships
Report. https://www.sponsorunited.com/insights/women
-sports-2022-report.

Brittaney Kiefer. (2025). "Nike's Super Bowl Ad Puts Women
Athletes Center Stage." *Adweek.* https://www.adweek.com
/brand-marketing/nikes-super-bowl-ad-puts-women
-athletes-center-stage-on-a-male-dominated-field/.

Wasserman's The Collective & ESPN Research. (2023).

Chapter 5

Michael K. Zürn, Fabian Buder, and Matthias Unfried. (2023). "Brand Purpose and Brand Success." *NIM Marketing Intelligence Review* 15, no. 1, 54–59. https://www.nim.org /en/publications/detail/markenzweck-und-markenerfolg.

burtsbees.com/blog/post/recycling-made-easy-2024/.

burtsbees.com/blog/category/impact/.

Chapter 7

ANA.net.

hallmark.com/crown-rewards/.

Americanexpress.com.

Andrew Barker. (2025). "Free Coffeee Pays Off for Star-bucks." *linkedin.* linkedin.com/news/story/free-coffee-pays -off-for-starbucks-6313276/.

Jonathan Maze. (2025). "Everybody Apparently Went to Starbucks on Monday." *Restaurant Business.* restaurantbusi nessonline.com/financing/everybody-apparently-went-star bucks-Monday.

Chapter 8

ANA.net.

Prada.com.

"Sea Beyond." pradagroup.com/en/sustainability/cultural -csr/sea-beyond.html.

Kristen McCormick. (2025). "76 Perspective-Broadening Stats About Diversity & Inclusion in Marketing for 2025." wordstream.com/blog/ws/2023/02/27/diversity-inclusion -marketing-statistics.

About the Author

GREG P. LICCIARDI is an Adjunct Professor at Fordham and Seton Hall universities where he teaches marketing and business strategy. Over the past ten years of teaching MBA and undergraduate courses, Greg has coined the term "Holy Grail of Marketing." It has become the core operating system that his students draw from when learning about and applying the latest trends in marketing.

Greg has held senior leadership roles at Worth Media Group, Elite Traveler, National Audubon Society, Univision, and American Express. He is currently Vice President of Sponsorships and Partner Programs at the Association of National Advertisers (ANA). In addition, Greg is an executive coach and is part of the Buccino Leadership Institute at Seton Hall where he mentors students.

Greg earned his MBA from Fordham University and his undergraduate degree from Rutgers University. He and his wife live in Summit, NJ, with their three boys. Beyond his passion for marketing, Greg enjoys fishing, cooking, and vacationing with his family on Cape Cod.

Share *Holy Grail of Marketing*. To order
additional copies for family, friends or employees,
go to www.holygrailofmarketing.com.